Reliquary Fever

New and Selected Poems

Beckian Fritz Goldberg

New Issues Poetry & Prose

New Issues Poetry & Prose
The College of Arts and Sciences
Western Michigan University
Kalamazoo, Michigan 49008

First Edition, 2010.

ISBN-10 1-930974-94-9 (paperbound)
ISBN-13 978-1-930974-94-4 (paperbound)

Library of Congress Cataloging-in-Publication Data:
Goldberg, Beckian Fritz
Reliquary Fever: New and Selected Poems /Beckian Fritz Goldberg
Library of Congress Control Number: 2010924164

Art Direction:	Barbara Loveland
Design:	Konomi Watanabe
Production:	Paul Sizer
	The Design Center, Frostic School of Art
	College of Fine Arts
	Western Michigan University
Printing:	McNaughton & Gunn, Inc.

Reliquary Fever: New and Selected Poems

Beckian Fritz Goldberg

New Issues

WESTERN MICHIGAN UNIVERSITY

Reliquary Fever: New and Selected Poems

Also by Beckian Fritz Goldberg

Body Betrayer
In the Badlands of Desire
Never Be the Horse
Twentieth Century Children (chapbook)
Lie Awake Lake
The Book of Accident

Sometimes the drawers of the earth close;
Sometimes our stories keep on and on. So listen—
Leave no address. Fold your clothes into a little
island. Kiss the hinges goodbye. Sand the fire. Bitch
about time. *Hymn away this reliquary fever.*

—David St. John

Contents

Lie Awake Lake (2005)

The Book of Accident (2006)

And One More New

New Poems

Shy Girls Waiting for You

When the god and I
began it was not with light
but with the dottle of the bird's
neck. After that I swore off

birds, those penitents, tight
sacks. While the god was
kneading his ball of dust
I watched the trees like TV

Land, waiting for the next
channel to alight. God,
I was a whore for a singing
detective, a Luminol

spray constellating the bed.
Still we continued and planted
the little beans that
unfurled like questions. Bit

by speckle by twang-twang
we covered a world and with one
finger a road and down the road
we put the sign
Shy Girls Waiting For You.

We conceived
the feeling of being caught in
the downpour in a strange
town without a raincoat. From there

we invented the human, hit
the bars blinking and the god
said, Let's die.

Genius,
I said and only then
did I think back,
back like a rabbit on fire

who can't know what it's like to be
put out, not at the moment

he is burning. It never
occurred to either of us to
think of miracles. People,
you are brilliant.

The god and I see double.
Beauty and hard beauty,
Oh,

hard, hard, hard.
Our questions are
our miracles.

Crocus

I wanted to stay in the earth:
There, I needed no skin—the dark
body was all around me.
I had no tongue. Above me, sleep,
a heaven of snow. Years,
years. Then the split,

the blue heart lifted almost
out—who was coming to save me?
How would I know myself, outside
self . . .

And then the sky. The you.
The first terrifying eye of a bird
coming down to me, a kiss
forced open. When I was buried

I did not need to forget. You
are what I need to forget
but not now—
not with everything in the air,
not with these lips
so designed to fail . . .

Twenty-First Century Pastoral

She had skin, and
from afar
the pink glow

of a dying town.
To be a man in
that town

you had to
hit the clubs,
pole-dancers in striped

bikinis, a guy
with a cowboy hat
strolling in. Life,

whatever stupid
cardigan he is,
slumming—

pay him no mind
as we never do
when we want to be happy

with the ink
in the small of her back.
That a bad life can be true

to its one pure thing
explains the gods
who are only muses

each of one discipline:
the naughty matchbook,
the wind,

what draws us out,
then in. Loss
is not a mystery,

ask the jukebox.
Ask your mother.
Blossom is where

you find it, the answer to
everything
leaving the body . . .

A flash of petals
above her tailbone,
the bottles above the bar

fluttering and light
like a field of zephyranthes.
Then to be gone

from that field, since anywhere
we once were
was possibly heaven.

Beauty and Truth

—for Maidi and Ike

Let me just say I'm a girl
who'd give her left nut to

know your name, sister,
sitting bowed beside your

pink drink. You so cool.
Let us go down to the world

where we blur, like butterflies,
into leaves & there's nothing

I wouldn't pretend for you.
I don't expect you

to be into my kink.
The body's always

changing. Tell me
are you the kind of boy

who can blush?
These days, longing's as big

as I get. You make me worry—
all gods take form

as their disguise. Then in strolls
some Clyde McFuck

a trace of hair in his
décolletage and you look up

with that sad sass of a smile.
I want you for a dream.

The dark one over there
can see it. His latest *amor* looking

as if he's bent on teaching
his cosmo to talk. Dark One

eyes some Trans-Lily,
née Lyle, slinking around, so pale

and deep. We're between-folk.
Permanently doppelgangered.

We cannot separate.
I'm back to you,

chimera in orange chiffon, breathing,
lush little hour before we all

go home. I don't know what you are. Me,

I'm part naiad.
But we have all refused love

some nights. There's no other proof
we have a soul. In this world where

everything that is beautiful
is random, there's no story.

We are like two hummingbirds that also never met.

The Metaphor of Gender

Why can't the boy be
named Rose, and why does the moon at all
enter into this—

It's the name he wants
in the next life.
I'll let you know when I get there.

In the literal meantime
swing to me my little sexamagig,

you have to believe the stronger
the more tender, you have
to be eaten upon capture like a code.

And why can't the rose be named
Vince, and (why are) his eyes
like falling into,

these shadows deep in the folds
of a velvet odor

fusing us to the world. And the moon—

it refuses to go away, a low
gold wedge tonight. Sexy?
You bet.

It eats its own flesh. Is death
a man in a robe with a scythe
or a woman with wings and
a loving potion?

Dear shining goon,
Alexander/Alexandra,
Alex, if I may call you—and may I

call you sometime?
I assure you I'll never leave
the body. Never leave
you for spring grass, that Millicent, or

for anything I can call Louise.
The gods are lonely. Tonight
the clouds glow like stars.
I know they are lonely.
Louise,

imagine, they call themselves lovers
but there's not a mark on them,
and they can't believe

when we say that boy is
like a soft quilt
embroidered with pears and

every seam unbroken
but one.

I See the Light Come Shining

My brother
came back
and shaved his head
and

left his wife. I got
a blouse tried on by
girls my age in

Saigon, so small
the black silk eyelets,
frogs, my mother said,

would not fasten
across me. The lavender
sheen like a dawn

somewhere so
far one could only
imagine

its girls, a field
hung from the
light itself.

From his wives
my brother had two sons
who both were suicides,

but the girls, all six,
lived. The sleeves
glowed in my closet

and then disappeared.
I thought as a girl
it was not my war.

Absence

It is where it isn't. For instance, the hallway. For instance, What next? The apple that says then I was happy, or I was happy then . . . When

you aren't here I don't have to make the bed. I don't have to eat on time. Well, hell, I'm just like memory and what good

does Papa do there? The red dog. The old house. The old baby. At least there's California where it's still possible to think while you

drive, stop, eat, watch the desert disappear and the flowers grow giant, conglomerate, famous and rich. I've been there, done

that. "Talk to me as if I were there . . ." said some clipping taped to the side of the refrigerator after

he was gone and I was back in my mother's kitchen, back at the mountain. He'd stopped the car so I could touch it before

the girl vanished into this. I was convinced I would feel the mountain under my hand as we rode into the desert from

the Midwest, from the snow and the year, farther and farther like an imagination. All left to conjuring. Reciting spells.

My palm flat against rough rock, the rest of the mountain didn't come, though I'd expected the whole to be

present. I knew you could feel an animal through its flank as you could a whole house through its quiet. But the mountain, a gray butte, wasn't

there. Present: some crackers, some olives, some ice, some booze. 8:30 and dark as the mouth. Talk to me as if. In the hospice where

my sister works there's a patient who speaks word salad. Not all gone quite yet. Not yet quite all gone. Come closer,

she gestures. Whispers, *I want to fill my husband up*. This is her nonsense almost.
Almost husband. Almost the shirt or when

or was I happy. If you can't bear to forget don't
be born.

Time is Happy

In my dream Keats lights another cigarette and coughs. He tells me in his dream he is
riding a horse, a horse walking slowly down the Via Condotti, and then he realizes it

is the horse his father fell from and died. The horse's dream I don't recall. And I
know nothing of what I speak but the slow walk

has begun and there are violets and one in the window which is a memory despite
everything. Here

everything but time digresses. Is so. I cannot say any god is happy. I cannot say
that time is happy. Awake,

I have not seen my father for ten years nearly to the day. Sometimes I so
wish that Sappho or Keats had said, *Tony drank club soda and said my skirt*

looked nice. Wouldn't that have helped us all? Oh, who wouldn't
make a soul if they could? Stop the car.

In the car each of us thinks of our century. The dog lights a Camel Red and sighs.
In the back

the family is stuffing itself with oranges from Mexico they can't bring back across
the border. Their hands sting and they eat standing

by the side of the road, the juice not even sinking into the pale dirt, but rounding
its little drops on the surface long enough to time—

20

21

one one thousand two one thousand . . . the station wagon doors
wide open. And so on.

To Sorrow

Twilight's scrubbing, scrubbing the whiteness of September's body
and the blue silt left on the roof somehow gets

from this minute to the next. If there is another world now
it will eat this one . . .

Space is coming out like the wary rabbit, like the creep of tenderness
back after the husbands have stopped shouting. I've come to

think now on the cool cinder block stacked
behind the house of exchanging new vows:
Let's promise to have the same argument all of our lives.
To imagine each other dead and then, imagining

sorrow,

say: Sorrow, do I know you, as only eyes could know
they could not be falling on any plusher twilight, on any
more motherly room, as only my drawn breath

could know the humic vinegars, chalk, the subtle
magnesias, musts of bark, of earth at home in this air.

Last night a woman flayed a man half
        to death in my dream and I wanted to save him

but stood by in my deep poise where it seemed I had
        a memory of kissing him or knew the future
        of kissing him, a stranger

who somehow now has gotten from last night to here.
What are we to do with our lives, tell me, whose language is
stay longer.

Everything is Nervous

How many days I can't think.
So when I do think of blue flowers
it's something to hang onto
something briefly phosphorescent.
To fill the void I watch endless
murders on TV. Potential suspects.
Can the bullets removed from
Vince's body reveal the identity of
the killer? How comforting is this
when I wanted to write a sonnet on mortality?

I remember my mother once planted
lilacs in a hedge. They aren't blue but
that's where my mind goes. The mind
being a nose.

Jojo, we have some questions to ask you,
says the cop.

Blue, the most grateful color.
Who could think of killing
the one they love. He, she. He and
he or she, she, or dog, sky. Suddenly

October cuts the endless summer cold.
But it's still the desert. Hardly green,
it's why I can't think, why the moon is
most at home here. You think it loves
those picturesque fields, those leafy
copses? Hard loves hard.

The air smells like cold iron tonight,
yes it does. It's something to
hang onto. Not like a thought.
Not like heroin in the suspect's pocket.
A secret life weirder than any
Little Rock detectives had ever known.
I bet in Little Rock they have flowers
blue as a blue bucket. Suspects, Suspects.

It's not a season if it expects
a conclusion. That's what I think,
because of you.

Apocrypha 114°

The heat is deafening
and obliterates distance
until all the panting
ghosts are here
haunting the water faucet,
baring their ectoplasm to
the hard-worked refrigerator.
Nipples galore rise
from the otherworld.
The fans churn and the open-mouthed
unlucky birds stuck
without relief scrap it out
over a few withered blossoms.
Fuck you, the world says.
I'm in here,
too sucked of love to dream.
For a few days a bobcat took
to sunning himself on the roof
of our house. So we prayed
as we entered and prayed as
we left. Fuck you,
sweet dry world, omen and
famine.

Vodka

The potatoes grow in an orchard
where the eyes are harvested by women in babushkas.
Its song is my song. It goes, *Let's paint
the town pink*. Followed by weeping.
When the belly is burning,
when the trees are bare, when the stray
horse runs around illiterate and happy
and the sun goes down like an olive
in ice, perhaps the melancholy
eats us to a person. And a man goes
home followed by women he doesn't even like.
That was my friend, Angel,
who stood in the leaves of his yard
among the Sleeping With. Sometimes
a certain century'd

talk to us, forgive our being
here and now, Jewish and
wasted, dancing to Johnny Cash.
It's old soul this thirst. Back to God.
Though the proof of anything is in
remembrance. The potato,
an apple, blinded by some fate.
Why isn't the body happy—
it has eyes, it has limbs, it has breath.
The town is blue, and white, and the leaves
sparkling . . .
And we, as Johnny says, *flushed*

from the bathroom of your heart.
Why can't we sing whatever we
want to sing to kill the mind, that pale
white doll, that piteous incursion
into Relationship. Shoes by the bed.
Into Super-Collider. Into Supermarket.
Followed by weeping. Talk to us,
Super Molecule, benevolent poison,
we are not what we want to be,
fruit of the earth.

Valedictory Shuffle with Accordion and Grapes

the light that bumps up some astonishing stairway

the blindness of grapes on a dish

the lumbering bird in the accordion

a painting can seem to go somewhere

a song is a going

the grape's translucent fingertip its whole body

nothing is unlike the weather

sun behind a cloud like the wet behind the skin

the accordion went on with the small restaurant

the point where light is almost like fog

you feel the dead hand of another parting

My Way, April Showers, That's Amore, Spanish Eyes

a painting of fruit on a painted table yellow behind the red

an accordion is the goose of pianos

oh, in that light my skin flamed up in partings

to see is to translate into memory

the grapes were suddenly blue in dark blue circles

shadow melting in E minor

a lake like silk clinging on the stairs

nothing is unlike the parting

the faces have been erased by the thumbs

in the restaurant/museum/vineyard

the accordion loses its breath and resuscitates

the light that leads you down the stairs

that, lover, is the scale and practice, practice

you pump another heart

the point where fog is almost like parting

the grapes painting somewhere in August

Extravagant

If this mouth wants to open like a plum and split
down your skin, suck in
the dark pit of you slick with
your golden birth-hairs and remember
its blossom, this tongue which wants to
prime itself in your mouth and
rhyme you with me like time

with money, it's because desire grows
more extravagant in silence, in waiting,
and the night-blooming cereus with its plumed
goblet, its paraffin luster, its perfect
party of subtle décolletage, offers itself
to June's neglect. It's punishment enough

passion's brief, desire long, form
traitorous, and the heart
good dog to all three. If the night wants
to return and return as it is, as a memory,

meanwhile this mouth can only say,
"What a warm night." "What a long summer."
This is how little
it can manage now. What a long summer

clung at the edge of the pool.
My father threw me in and I swam to him,
threw me in and I swam to him.
It was as simple as I thought
longing would be.

Yet what a warm night, and the mouth
is not mouth enough. It wants
to be a nocturnal industry.

It wants to build a bomb with you.

It wants to be the village
and surrender and surrender you

to me,
whom I was born to torment.

Leda (2)

To hell with women.
They who rescued me from the swan's song,
they who turned me

out of the old need to
measure immeasurable longing and plumbed me
like an excuse

for every kind of pious
earth-motherly sociologic gyno-kitsch
imaginable.

Some sisters.
They don't want to hear love
is about boundaries,

even a god who says *now*
will spend the rest
of his flighty everlastingness

singing *then*. I want to go back
go down . . .
What's the punch of ravishment
if it doesn't drop us?

What Has He Done

Someone's jammed
a paper cup in the grip of the flowering vine. That's it

for the day. The vine goes on
adoring itself. If it were a man
you'd say, "There's a man who's lucky in sorrow,"

and dusk sets off
another round of silly karaoke from the birds.
Riffs and dies, riffs

and dies. Into this ice,
gin. No lemon. Zero hour. And aching.
Until everything's the wince of a bruised eye.
What's hurt

to love? What's a rock to honey? What's regret?
Someone's sorry,

someone's through. I love this Sea Breeze
Motel slumped in the dark. I love you, mister,
upstairs tranced

by the beam of the Spice Channel on TV. You,
sister, pinching the bikini by its black strings from
the black rail of the balcony. When I'm

on sparrow-watch like this, sad watch, I forgive you all—
but I am going, any minute, to report

that couple arguing in the pool. The woman
wailing, *you, you.* At the radium edge,
the half-man in the water puts his finger to
his lips. So no one throws shoes at them.

What has he done. Shh. What—

There's a man who's polite
in misery. In the garbled blue underlight,
ruff of the footlight pinned to the trunk of a queen palm.

Her head's bowed. She's gone simple
as the sound of a nail pried from a board
into this story. Into this
half-life. Ssh.

I want her to leave him.

Float. Hear the blinds click. Water sleep.
We came here to get away.

We were tearing ourselves apart.
We were doing ourselves violence,
like other lives were possible.

Blown

Have you lost your mind, are you wingstruck,
is there a piece of you gone, why can't
that fire fall out of your chest or are
you completely unstrung with the stripping
him down to the hot quick of you and
too lamentably eyesick, voicesick, breastsick
to understand there's no hope for you—
you must be lightdead, you must be socket
blown, heartshot, blinded by doves
and he will not know you ever
he will not think suddenly of you, or one day
say, touch. Look, anything outside of your
intoxicated shine to yourself, such a maddening
monkey, are you out of your head, are you
off your nut, have you taken leave
of your senses, are you not all there,
is something loose, gone soft—
are you beyond mercy, is he
a scent with no source in the house,
is he kind to you in dreams, is his throat a place
for you to die, unpardonable, ludicrous, bedazzled,
do you hear voices, do you see benevolent
forms, do you think you've been stabbed
and now you're standing over the body
not yours—not his—but the body
drunk, drunk up again, have you entirely
lost touch, do you have roses for brains,
do you live on the moon
that his oblivion waxes you, easy pearl,
are you all balled up, have you come
unhinged, woman,
is anyone home?

Wound Man: Apologie and Treatise

1. *The Whole Gun*

When the light in all its original lateness has reached
through the spindly chaparral and made a moon
of just this much quartz dust and pebble, appearances
are everything:

Wound Man arrives, all the skin torn from his buttocks
which makes it hard to walk. But the *obturator externus*
glistens. It feels the rush of air as a tongue might.

He is working on bedsores. It is his life's work.

I know that pain is a laboratory. Just like a violet.
A certain amount of light added or
subtracted, a certain placement

in time in time. On a string across the window
my grandmother would hang the wishbones of chickens.
In the sill she kept a violet that by now is

almost incandescent. The *gluteus maximus*
rides over the greater trochanter of the femur. Look
the marbling blues and garnets and the crown
of pus where the infection bored through . . .

No, I can't keep my mind on anything:

He also
has a needle in his genitals. And he is lying down,
now, in the prodigal twilight. The whole desert
glittering like a smashed bottle. Here,
we can't even plant trees. We have to jackhammer them
in. This body,

though, leaks light, it measures its bag of light. It will
give it to science. And it will land on a lake
going either way, way of the wavering underbird
locked breast to breast with the solid drake.

Take longing close

to what it wants and the whole gun goes through you
with the shot. Wound Man has come from the north
with a pistol jammed to his head and his head
dreaming of violets and his mouth full of blood.
Part of the skin is missing—
but this ain't personal.

2. *Lullaby*

Everything is a look. A gash.

Don't look at the thing. Look at the look.

Why do we love to watch someone sleeping?
Why do we soar then with power
and tenderness?

As now, even the cup is soaring, left
on the windowsill where the ephemeral damasks
of the bougainvillea blossoming outside
bespell the form. At least

that's what I saw. No penetration.
Every eye stopped by something. Like you,
I've found my own eye beautiful in that
nervous mirror eye—the color of woodsap,
and flecks of green horsedung, deerfly,
little specks burnt by a match, and a halo
of lilac, yes, lilac.

It isn't a pomegranate and it isn't a honeycomb.
Could be a fish. Could be the gillwork of the undersea
mushroom.

I don't think anything is about language at all.
Language looks.

Maybe an anemone in the tidepool. The green

submarine fringe is from my father's eye. Lit up.
Its own little eager kitten. Its own bright beetle.

Copper, too.
A surreal line of midnight blue around the iris.

My brothers showed me a trick when I was four:
They rolled up their eyelids
so the red wet underside showed and they rolled
the eyeball back in their heads
until it was white, and the little red lightning
of the veins—

and these were my brothers dead. Zombies.
And I remembered them.

3. *The Work*

Wound Man appears, a gunshot in his head,
a nail through his eye, an arrow in his shoulder,
a knife in his gut, a dog bite on his right
ankle, a thorn in his left thigh, a bruise on his ribs,
a musket ball in his left calf, and an icepick in his neck.
He has been this way since the sixteenth century.

He is chewing parchment plants to stop the flux
of mouth-blood. He will apply a poultice of ground
crocus flower to the knife wound. He will need
instructions for getting the arrow shaft out.
He will practice debridement.

He will put leeches on his ankle. He will cauterize
the calf with boiling oil and cause infection.
He will rub his thigh with laurel beans. He will cure
nothing by prayer,

Christ is nothing. A few holes. And the palms
are tough. The ankles, too. So when, as they say,

he came back perfect, it was all appearance. But
Wound Man stayed with the work

of body. A bee stung his armpit. A stone
hit his skull and he bled. The eye, well, the eye
couldn't be saved, and gangrene began in his leg
again, and the lash torn across his back
began to heat. Up like praise.

4. *Ankle's Own Soul*

Wound Man is bleeding from the bear trap
which his ankle drags around. It doesn't matter
at this point that he's not a bear. Alive
is as intelligent as it gets when torment
is involved. It doesn't matter at this point
that he's not bleeding from a hammer blow.
Or a fast bus. Wound Man is working on a potion
made from berries and leaves to clot the blood.
He is looking for a tool to loosen the trap,
but not enough tool sheds in the woods.
Plenty of angels. Sure, they're all over him
and the state of his soul. *What is the state*
of your soul? they ask.

Soul don't say.

His ankle is throbbing and his sweat is cold.
He is awaiting the miracle of endorphins
which he's heard often occurs near death.
But the gnat-angels, the gnat-angels—he can't
brush them all away. They swing in
his delirium, soul, soul, soul. He wishes
he were a bear. But his soul is fine.

Really. Though the teeth are in him deep

and the mouth is hard on the flesh and the spring
the little rusty spring of the trap . . .
Only mind would do this, make a trap.
body wouldn't do this to body—

Wound Man's mauled ankle begins to circle heaven.
Yes. A heaven where the limbs go,
the smashed arm, the diabetic leg, the sawed off
fingers. *No soul in them.*

The gnats say something, he is sure. Something
like thrown knives. Something like flying glass.
Something like fire singeing hair. While he tries
to pry the teeth of the trap apart with an abandoned
shovel blade and a strong stick. And then

he'll drag himself away. And dress his ankle,
daily, like his own little child, pale and still,
except for the teeming face.

5. *Half Paradise*

The mouth looks for itself
in another body. It looks
for the perfect match, dark space, deep
breath. Mouth
is this half of paradise

this split-winged fire beetle—

What will fill it? What will suck it from itself?
What will save us from the body?

the mouth looks out for itself—
let bones do what bones do. The flightier
beauties of the night are moving: the lizard
walks the window screen and the burrowing

owl rises. And the mouth sips water

by the bedside. When it dreams the kiss
is not yours, it is the doctor's who scraped
my blood out, it is the idiot son's of a neighbor
who scared me as a child. His lips
are tight, like the tied balloon.

Mouth has been holding its breath
when I wake. Thank the dark.

The first kiss, long ago, was to its own
arm—long and hard—imagining
it was not an arm.

6. *Metaphysic*

When the blood appeared above his left breast
he could not remember where it came from.
He closed his eyes and tried to recall if something
had ripped out his heart. Was it there?
Or something was driven in.
There was nothing to substantiate—

Some days we wake up changed
and can't recall the changing.

The final December light on the brittlebush,
the olives silvering above their wells of gravel,
and the coxcombs of fuchsia above the autumn sage
fit the desert quietly. It always has
the look of abandonment, this desert. The look
of something the body has just left—a sheet, a scene, a bed,
a room, a horizon . . .

But Wound Man can't pin down the cause of blood
this time. He hadn't run into a sword.
He hadn't fought a man with a broken bottle.
He hadn't been in a car accident.

He hadn't been in the hospital.

But there was a hole in him.
And the hole was bloody, half-clotted, and hot.

Had something tried to eat him?
Was there such a thing as a vampire worm?
Or was it a crow, straight for the meat?

Like a blue torch,
the sky through the tree

and him the soaked rag burning.

7. *Spring*

Because grief can be resurrected.
Because the gash of scent or the stab of flower.
Because time blooms time.

Because March begins again.
Because morning glories and snap beans.
Because swoon is the name of everything today,

false spring in January, a balm and lush
light, the body thinks it is spring. The honeysuckle
starts to bud against the west wall.

All my life the desert has taught me this trick.
It is Spring:

He has fallen from a ladder
and landed on an old board with a nail in it.
The nail has opened his shin like a bright fish
shining gut.

He does not remember the stitching up
or the pulling out.

He remembers only April, ripping
the bandage off with its leg hairs and the sting
and the pink crust, the good skin around it
pallid, damp, gleaming with salve.
Necrotic rose.

Because even so the story is only
part of the story.

8. *At the Grave of Odysseus*

I have found it. The little plot
at Kamiros among the aleppos, the rip
of the cicadas so that the place seems
enchanted by unholy frequencies that
mount the ear and then unmoor the heart.
All the stories of his end are wrong.
That is the nature of story, to put an end
to the unending, to feed us time in
gobbets. My nostrils were lit
with the fragrance of pitch, the warm
pine bark, the clear air. Cliffs, all around
this place. A man riding the road with
the head of a motorcycle and the rump
of a truck. The centaur of fumes.
What I have found is the hero of journey
fallen. By now he is bone and all
the wounds have vanished. The grove
smells heavenly and, beyond, the sea
damasks itself with lapis and iolite, with
bright bruises. *Mercy me I can't tell you
how my heart is broke.* The great matters
of the world swell and crush but the grave
where I leave a pebble, that is for
the man most loved for his return. It was not
his face but the scar on his foot the loved ones
recognized. Now *there* is a story, I thought.
Whatsoever that means.

9. *The Lute*

John Donne once said the twitching body
of a decapitated man was like a lute's strings.
This is what Wound Man loved about
the Metaphysicals. They knew their anatomy.
They knew that beauty was another
pestilence that ran its course and that poetry
alone could molest desire. They did endless
experiments: One in which they lifted a house
into the body of an ox, then a whole country, India,
its incense and exotica, into the body of a woman.
What this proved, they never told. Of course,
it was death they were trying to beat. If they
could just beat the body. But the body always
trumped: *My apple better than your apple,*
My shine more than your shine.
My kung fu better than your kung fu.
They were left alone with words, but
what was speech in a book of murder?

10. *Anatomia Fugitiva*

The first scar was from birth, the scar
of the umbilicus, in the center of his body.
It was like a blond spider curled in death.
It was the little wheel that froze . . . From there
to everywhere was far enough. Next
came the wound from the hot flame he touched
and the dogbite in the pure flesh of his forearm.
Then the pox. It's how his body told time.
It was June. The desert bright as salt.
Not a shadow. Not one. The great stand-off.
But how he got here was a mystery, as
solitude always is. Between the signs in the story
and the leap . . . What next? The white waxen
belltowers of the yucca raise a crowd of

old joys in him. The wasp thinks him through.
The mesquite stiffens the sexual hair, and
the dry wash glittering with tin cans—that
must be for the intestines. Everything, he saw,
having its place, like a good arrow.

11. *Pastoral*

The conclusion: Every body has
a wound that is secret. When he
goes to work they can't see the one who goes
to sleep, who drifts off seeing the small chicks
the farmer used to carry in a flat, like marigolds.
Everybody thinks what they see is what they get.
His secret wound is like being a woman,
he thinks. And when a man thinks of being a woman
he thinks of being helpless, or wicked. This
is the wound he doesn't dress—

there are reasons to be naked inside one's self,
a bell the flesh claps—

always one can hear the self, far away
like the countryside in a postcard

and I stand still like a resemblance.

Body Betrayer (1991)

Revolution

Like the curve of the body
that rises only in sleep,
light in November. I unwrapped the bells
of new wine glasses tucked with tissue paper,
folds of great worry smoothing
to the floor. Behind in the window
the tiger eye of autumn. I could
smell the visitors coming with fruit baskets
and scribbles of violets.
And then the glasses were standing
in a clear row, so it remained
only for a small transparent man to walk
his crystal spaniel along that boulevard.
I was, for a moment, almost a sphere.
Then the sour streak of your mouth
cursing the way I kept a house.
And a sheet tented the floor,
a remnant shade of some dream
last night, crease like an orchid.

What a man can say now
to a woman he loved this morning
is like finding the earth revolves
around a fly. Tonight the edges
of me part and float like brides,
like ghosts, one in the piano bar
on the late show, one drowsing over the cool
fringe of the cat, one in some other year
where the schoolyard is whiskered with frost,
the pink moth glowing
huge on the east wall . . .

I have heard of countries where revolution
has broken out over an old broom,
its hairshock of silence. Where heads
come off because the moon dizzies
in the shoemaker's wine.

It is too much for one body.
Lying down as darkness sheets
the eye violet. Waking in the morning
with the sadness
of opening a gift alone.

Geraniums

My husband does Jolson in the kitchen.
My father-in-law at 81 has taken up
telling dirty jokes—interrupts
to tell them, or to mention did we know
most people die in March. But today
he stands in the garden he built
complete with ceramic frogs in pools, and talks
about sperm, how marvelous it is.
That each time a man ejaculates he releases
thousands, and out of those thousands
in a thousand times, one
makes it. Nearly blind in one eye,
diabetic, his balance cloudy, he leans
against the planter and says
what a miracle of odds it is
to be born. Squints out at the sky.
My husband croons *rockabye* from the kitchen.
The trumpet flowers suck at his father's white sleeve.
She always makes me get dressed up, he says.
But where the hell am I going?
We sit. And the light just stays
the way it always would if we could make it.
Over the pink geraniums
a bee sounds like thousands.
I breathe the pony odor of peat,
a trace of chlorine. Watch
the way the water
returns through the clay frog's lips
and jiggles the sky. Think
of the odds against this . . .

Salvation

A helicopter's shadow pinwheels
on the canyon floor. Wild burros
are inclining just the distance from one another
friends do, when presence
but not touch
is the right consolation. Surely

there is a reason these things
make a world: The Colorado curves
the famous textbook set of parallel lines
that will meet at infinity.
As we watch from the rim
a silver beating in the dry grasses,
the halo of the chopper's descent,
all space changes like the nap of velvet.

Through binoculars we read
the mouths of burros
who must be calling out something
it took them a long time to learn.
Airlifted above the rest, one
hangs calmly in harness, bobs his head
slowly as if to say yes, yes . . .

We know the story of Icarus is not true.
Dumbest damn creatures, the ranger says.
Don't even look up.
They pay no attention to the mother copter
bearing the gray burro from point A
over the lips of the mesas, up
toward the white cattle trucks
clustered at point B. They remain

bent to the weeds
that burst in rock, medieval alchemists
hard at study, while in the air
the genius of them makes
a new assumption. This morning
one by one they discover
the coming of an age.

Yet even as they are moved they forget
and, miles away on new plateaus,
will resume their old beliefs
in the magic of fissures, in the luck
of the foot, in scent the bridegroom   ♪
hesitating
at the hollow of the scented . . .

Already they recall only distantly
rising in harness,
as we do falling in dreams,
staring out as the trucks rock
down Highway 66
their eyes holding
the kind of picture we have
when we are not ourselves.

Emerson's Walk to a Shaker Village

The heat of summer came
like a wound from a friend. Spiders
touched a web to a thornbush
by the gate, and tiny shadows pooled underneath
the gentians. He wrote, *the days of September*
saturate, and walked
past the shiftless pig farms, 20 miles, to Stow

then Ashburnam. All night he'd felt the reach
of sweat. Now he was far,
a whole day's walk. His house, that nothing,
like a seashell far inland
was always settling. That morning
while the good Sisters readied breakfast

the Brethren gave an honest account
of their faith. Cloutman showed him
the vineyard, the orchard, the herb-room.
The grapes were both white and Isabella,
the orchard dumb with shape. He thought,
this capitalist is old and never dies.

In that shade he felt his father's hand
on his neck, forcing him into the water
off some wharf or bathhouse,
and wanted to hide as he used to
in Aunt Mary's prayers.
He liked to imagine her mind,

its infinite Himalayan folds.
He told his friends, the world
is awakening to union
like a crocus under snow. And that day
if Hawthorne had not been inclined to pontificate,
and he himself with a cold, and if
they could have stayed 24 hours
he might have convinced

the Shaker farmers to awake, to propagate.
They showed humor.
They appeared to understand
the idea of union, the second crop.

Cutting Worms

As all children, he learned of it—
this strange ability to receive the cut

and go on living like two
worms shrugging across the soil.

This delighted him. The self
was endless and he proved it

slicing the earthworm
gray as a laboratory liver.

How odd it was
a brain without location

like God, or Joseph the accountant's son
when his heart stopped,

who became two Josephs, one cool
as his finger in mud

one still dancing on top of his bicycle,
grinning.

The grin the worm wears
is its whole body

flexing over lantana roots,
quartz grains like grooved roads.

When it is severed
with a spade or a jackknife

it rolls and glistens and becomes
them, two worms parting from

a point in the dust
as if they agreed to it.

They are not capable of pain,
they are like girls' ribbons

or the saints whose greatest virtue
his teacher said

was to be disinterested.
He understood

the soul was like this,
not in any part

and so dumb
that you could shred a man

with a razor blade
as leaves' shadows sometimes slit open

his face, and never find it.
He was not after it:

He would sometimes halve a worm
on the chair of a swing

to show the others
and give the new pair

names, and wonder
if they ever met again

and knit like true skin,
slick and whole as grace.

He could not imagine it
any other way.

Old Countries

Last night your father was tired and sang
the old Russian song, *Sing, little songbird,*
sing. You are a dumb son of a bitch.

Early, before light, you lay awake
wondering why he never told you before
about his cousin from Lithuania
who taught him to sing, about the grandfather
who won the lottery and bought a horse
that had cancer and died. Rivka, your grandmother
with the heavy eyebrows, kept all the money
after that. You try to picture the man you met
only once, when you went with him
to get a pack of Chesterfields
and he bought you a little boat.

You can never find them
because they changed their names
when they came over on the ship.
As the story goes, your name
came from the man ahead of them,
a peddler from East London.

But then there's Uncle Chanya's tale
that your grandmother was never sent for
from the old country, and came anyway
on her own, and found her husband
with a sick race horse. She believed in names.
She could find the one wolf
in all New York: Your grandfather,
the pin peddler, whose name was Bill.

Your father couldn't explain how she found him,
not if the story of the name was true.
And if it was not, how did she know the people
would still be there where the names
had left them? So he says there is another story

that the relatives in the old country
got sick of her, a manless woman,
a wigmaker's daughter, no good to matchmakers.
Useless, they said, useless as a hat
on a dog. In those days the country, he said,
was full of fools and dogs

but they had a logic about leaving.
Someone would start talking of a place
where you could get rich, eat meat
on weekdays. *Hok mir a chinik,*
the others would say.

But your grandmother came, and later
your father's cousin who taught him
the old song. And she told him a story
that she had a first name
but that it had changed
when she nearly died of diphtheria at ten.
No one remembers it.

Last night when your father was tired
he told you the same old story:
That his father had come from there
and bought a horse. Its sides
began to crease with bone,
its eyes began to ring
with delicate concave shadows.
After six years he had written his wife,
sent her part of the money, saying
there was more. Your father was not born yet.

But there was a child
who had died in the old country
whom they never spoke about. That was how
she knew how to find him.
Uncle Chanya claimed her at the dock
because your grandfather had some business
in the country. With a carrot he led

the little gray ridge of horse out in the snow
and shot it.

The horse's name was Malkeh.

State Street Motel

The wallpaper is full of larkspurs
which halve and curl at each seam. You lie on the bed.
The mirror holds a precise dark mouth
where the tip of the closet door is open.
I am watching you and thinking
how we took a train to get here
through snow, the tiny curtains that parted
New Haven, White River, Montpelier Junction.
It was two hours late, and then somewhere
outside a town, swelled to a stop.
The lights blotted off
the shapes of passengers' heads
all along the car, the crackle
of someone stepping on a candy wrapper. Inside
our window, a birch's comb, glazed,
and the snow's seals, broken and pasted back
over footprints. Everyone whispered. But now
there's nothing louder than two suitcases
set neatly in a corner of this room, a day

where snow on the hills lifts like thin paper.
I am writing this down because I don't understand
anything about us. In this room, a bed, a blanket
flipped over like a leaf of a calendar:
In April there's always a picture of a meadow,
a quote from Wordsworth, a holiday
for fools. Your curled hand is emptying exhausted ponies
from the edge of the bed
onto the hard yellow carpet. I'm here
watching you sleep because six years ago
we promised each other something.
We were married outdoors. I can't remember
the last time I stayed awake this long.
The snow outside you falls,
light the January sky tears up. What is this place?
When do we arrive? Maybe
the dreams that keep us going
are no better than our lives.

Maybe it hasn't turned out like this.

First Love

At night we'd haunt the bleachers' back row. Out there
was the center of something, baldness
quietly taking hold in the grass. Moths against
the stadium light like torn up notes.
When the traffic died some nightbirds
stuck in citrus along MacDonald Avenue
would whistle once at the silence, something
you forget nightbirds ever do, until they do.

I'd heard a story once about a flyball gone foul
and denting in the dark blue roof of someone's Pontiac
parked in the lot of Queen of Peace Church.
I used to wonder if a person could be killed
that way, walking casually toward downtown
by the right field fence.

In 1971, love was like that,
falling where the body was and where
the wind carried: though he was short
and asthmatic. I stood there like one of the Mexican kids
on car bumpers waiting for some hard swing to send one
over, hollering, *This one's mine*. And then
they'd scramble and elbow one another for it
like the whole safety of the free world
depended on this. But at night they were gone

and it was different, hollow, and he'd sit
a long time without speaking. I'd wait a long time
for something I believed he was going to say.
Once I put my hand
inside his shirt, feeling the strange cloudiness of hair.
Spring air from the field sank
like cooled coffee, a stone in shade.
I remember thinking I'd remember this
and it would come to me later on its own

when I'd just be walking casually at night
to lock the back door, or sitting down
to write a letter, deciding to whom . . .

The Flamingo at the Palo Verde Nuclear Plant

Who can say how
the lost get as far as they do. Suddenly
above the waste water lake his current
softened with forgiveness. The guys on break
shook their heads and grinned.
It was almost like before a holiday

when work goes easily, the hand half-in
another life. There was a gathering:
a few reporters, the foreman, a secretary
from the Audubon. The water flocked with light.

The bird strolled then, corsage on stilts. Or
a model on the beach, striking
each pose for a long time, long enough
to think what to do first
in the New World . . .

Helicopters swiped their arcs
in the air, dropped cargo nets and dragged
nothing, intersected and abstract
as plans for grief.
Slivering his blush wings
to his black tailfeathers, he found
their margin of error, crossed
the length of the water
over and over

with the new evening. It was almost
a ballet. Or who could say
what. When I was a kid it was jackrabbits
standing up in traffic
like someone called them. As always

no one expected a history of this.
The flamingo lighting with his wings
kept open could have been saying
grace, while the men whispered *son-of-a-bitch*
and *how'd he get here* . . .
feeling a bit sorry, but perfect, as one does

about a thing that has to be done.

Spring

Outside, the mouths of your horses tear
down to the white of the grass.
The cottonwoods end.
Day drops with the clean sweat
of candles. In the room men are clouding
your death with flesh, murmuring
about the hairlike quality of your hair; how strange
finding the bruised gray couch without you.

All around me the small vibrations
of your name pass from lip to lip
while in the kitchen the tops of cakes
wrinkle, grow cool
and the young priest like a beautiful
black tent
sits in the wind of the oven.

A light square rests in the wallpaper
where the mirror was removed this morning.
Young colts are understanding
the swirled face of water
in the tin trough
behind the house.

Dusk releases every shape. Cut flowers
catch in the windows.
Your cool fingers reach out
· and print the air as though it were a goblet.
Grief is the second life. The priest's skirt
pours over and over again like wine.

The Perception of Motion

First he dropped two iron balls,
the light one and the heavy one,

from the tower, at the same instant.
A pigeon went on overhead

chintzed with light.
He did not have to wait long:

A peasant rolling a wagon wheel
down the stone street

let it go ahead of him
and part two priests

walking from the baptistery, their cassocks
rising about the height of the chickens.

Then the wind dropped.
The wheel fell against a nut merchant's stall.

The balls clacked
on the ground like two beads,

one sound. He carried them home
and wrote, *two round objects*

of different weight will fall
at the same speed, straight.

But it was hard to describe
as that moment for the peasant

when the quail shot in flight
shuddered and moved back

and dropped in an arc
behind him

reddening the field grass.
Each word reflects belief

about the motion
it stops. This was most difficult

for the priests
who held Galileo *heretic*

yet could not deny
such a being

moved forward as he fell—
just as the spring water that year,

in Pisa, received its impetus
from river ice

that had carried it slowly
toward release.

The peasant, Giorgio, the vine-tiller
who could not write

would have told them
there were tiny animals of God

in wine, that tunneled
like ticks into his red feet,

but he was lucky.
That year, as any other,

snow fell, the dog's teeth
knew the plush of quails' necks . . .

Sometimes he missed
and all the field birds rose

at once, in the same direction,
and revolved.

It was hard to explain the good
of the invisible,

as talking to his daughter at night
he thought of many things

but only told her one.

The Children Dream Death

The boy is sitting in the closet cutting off
the heads of dolls to send back to Russia.
His mother's in the kitchen licking the backs
of stamps which gleam like fever. This is how
it begins. In the window of his bedroom
a garbage truck drives up and the men grab
his parents and stuff them in. The devil,
red tail crooked with the poise
of a phonograph arm, hisses, If you tell,
if you tell . . . The next evening at the dinner table
his mother says, What's wrong with him.
He doesn't eat. He begins to cry and confesses
everything, the dolls and the truck and
the garbage and the devil. All night
he trembles for them to come.

It is midnight and the girl
shops with her mother. They load the cart
with packages of frozen broccoli, corn,
and next is her father lying peacefully
in the shredding wings of frost above
the freezer case. The tips of his brown shoes
sugared with ice. His arms folded.
She cries to her mother, Look, look,
then the furniture and the silence
the nightlight in the hallway come see.

The house is familiar but wrong.
The boy's mother is saying, It's time. We
were told to pack our toothbrushes.
His father says, Now we'll be leaving.
There's yellow carpet in the doorway
like bad light. They're dressed for a day
on the patio, a trip to the bank.
It's time, they say, we'll just
take our toothbrushes and be
going. He can't stop them

because they are so simple. He wakes up
and the moon floats its blank head
over roofs in darkness which does not
speak English, though it has lived here.

Visiting the Stockyards

Behind the splitrail fence, a few bulls step
crushing shadows into their own manure.
Our white hands curve neatly over the rails.
They are surrounded. The teachers lean in red sweaters
near a gate, and over us
the cattle's voice breaks, ragged
and in great hunks. It's May
and the foreman leads us slowly toward
the crusted walls of two barns, lit
by a break in the clouds like a small village
under a dome of glass.
In the bulls' eyes it is always night.
Kept for breeding, he says. They
grown heavy gazes in front of us
like stonewort blooming in deep ponds.
This morning men wear gloves like oven mitts
and herd a brown steer from the mud,
past a metal gate, into a corridor,
and other men wait, dressed in bloody smocks.
When the blade flashes in the stall,
its cud pours out like milk, full of slivers.
Over the hills, there's a little cache of rain.
Its legs fold twice: the knees bend
and hesitate, as if from some sudden
recollection, then crush on the floor.
Some of the young girls
have shut their eyes, but over the hills
the sky's a sheer nightgown
showing the flesh where darkness
has set its tiny seam. And, in their yard,
the heifers pull slowly apart
staring at something else
vacant, like new widows
with someone who says he's a friend.

The Cloud by Desire

It is day in the movie,
night here,
and they have submarined north
testing

invisible fallout. It is days after
the end of the visible world.
Already ghosts

these men underwater, pale
as the screen's daylight
projecting on us, tones and shapes

of San Francisco Bay.
The periscope reads
its blank docks, still streets—
one crewman's home town,
so he has to have a look.

Through the hatch he escapes
for shore, and they are calling to him:
God's Gregory Peck voice
through the surfaced megaphone
calling to him who wants
to die at home.

When the captain dreams it is daylight
it's never here, but north
where he was born. Though he's
never returned, the barns

are still pitched, the gas cans
oxblood with rust. The cows
in winter
with saliva freezing
on their muzzles, melting
with their next breath . . .

Place has its advantage over them
like the body. No one's

content to end
in the Mexican cancer clinic,
the Swiss miracle spa.
When they finally give up
it's for home.

That's why
these sailors return to harbor
and, when the sickness comes,
forget their last moment love affairs
and go north again
to nothing

but the idea of nearness:
There is a field of corncribs
and a silo. A bridge. Sky
with its tangerine streak.
The grocery stores

are open. The horse standing,
the grass moving. A cloud
by desire.

And day there . . . night here.

Horses at Estero Beach

Tonight I want to believe they're still
waiting on the uneven sand and staring
out onto, or over, the blue abstraction
of ocean. And some of them
with the mattered eyes flies love, and some
showing like old brass in the sun
and beside them the Mexican boy with his open shirt
hoping we will change our minds
and be the day's first customers. But we only look

and imagine the movies—
I remember Brando on his way, riding
to see the sheriff's Mexican daughter.
You remember Becket and the King
shouting above the cold English coast.
And they will always ride like that, as long
as there are waves

and late night television, washing
the bed with silver
like an old love we can still see
but from a distance
and in a sadder light. Then, we just kept moving

toward the crippled edge of the bay,
carrying our shoes, jeans rolled up
on our white legs. And everywhere our feet
pressed on the wet sand, small ashen auras
spread and vanished. I guess neither of us
felt like being in the movies, caught
in the soft frames of the wind
because we said nothing. We stood
by the ocean looking back
at the desolate patios of the hotel,
the air the color of wet paper
above the violet open lips of bougainvillea.

That night you put warm wet towels
on my puffed stomach where our child
used to be. And we didn't close the curtains
but watched the moonlight

and someone crazy sat out on the pier
trying to fish. And others came back late
turning their keys and laughing
and dropped their shoes.

Then I listened to your breathing
so I wouldn't hear my own.
I was planning to dream of those horses
moving slowly as the boy led them home.
I don't remember if I did.
But I think of them often,
their curved bellies, their smooth flanks, and ribs
molded over their bodies like sand
on sand.

Tonight I want to tell you they're out there
shapely and dark with waiting
and it would have been so easy
though, by now, I think the boy knows
we're walking up under the shade of the cabanas
and up the steps, receding, and we're never
coming back. The mares are watching
the last scene in the world, sand and water,
as if it's an empty screen. Maybe
they lie down slowly and breathe.

As if the sky were a warm damp towel
growing cool.

In the Badlands of Desire (1993)

The Possibilities

After a wife's death a man may talk
to his horse with a great tenderness
as if, just this morning, he had tried on
her pink slipper. And if he has no horse
he may crack this window a little
wider when it lightly rains to confirm
the roofs and trees are made
of paper. If there is no rain
he may make himself a meal at midnight,
sweet artichokes and Danish cheese,
a glass of red wine. If there is
no red, then white. He may suck the knife
clean with his tongue. Later

lying awake he may hear the wild lung
of a motorcycle far off on a far road.
If there is no motorcycle, a dog
trying for any syllable in any known
language. Something falling suddenly in
the closet, according to some law.

Nearness in the dark is a kind of beauty
though it is only a lampshade, a shoulder
of the walnut chair. If there is no chair,
then a shelf. A shelf of books with the devil's
violet fedora tossed on top. Or something
exotic from the sea, manta ray

like the pulse in the ball of his foot.
A man may walk ten steps behind
his life. It may be sorrow or fear.
He may see her back like two doves rushing
up where a boy has flung a handful
of pebbles. If no pebbles, leaves
where a masked prowler hunches, his belt of
lockpicks, his bag of velvet like the one
from which memory snatches. These are
the possibilities, the immaculate

like miracles which are nothing
in themselves, but in this world a sign
of angels, ghosts, supernatural beings
who watch us. Who listen. Who sometimes
helplessly let us stumble on
their pyramids, their crude observatories
or let us, generation after
generation, speak to the broken horse
of the human heart.

Black Fish Blues

I've got a cigarette and a bee outside my window.
The window is dusty, speckled like an old pear skin.
I've got a cleaning woman coming once a week,
a pomegranate tree with its red bomber lips

ticking the wind quiet outside. Wind
you can see but not hear. I've got a cup
of coffee and hours the size of my palm.
A cup of coffee and the taste of muddy water

stubbing my teeth. Muddy water like the child in me
finds in her dreams. I don't know why I go there.
Bee with its striped brain loves the curl
light shaves in the air. Curl you can follow but

not see. I've got a view and a neighbor with a drainpipe
running off his roof. I've got a feel for the plumbing
broken in those shadows. I've got May light
coming in strong on all stations and branches

knocking their shadows flat on the blocks of the fence.
I've got a whole cluster of black fish bobbing
in the top block. Fish that touch you quick
constellations below the water. I remember this.

I've got a third hand and a third leg, another
skin that remembers things. I've got that leg
halfway up the road I'm walking with my sister
in the snow of '58. There's the body of a rabbit

trapped beneath the ice. There's the marble
of stillness and shadow. It's a long way
to the heart of our house. It's a long way,
sister, to here, my good legs crossed

as I sit in my chair. I've got shoes
waiting over in the corner like I've died.
Red shoes that go with nothing I own.
They've got their heels near each other

for conversation. I'm talking about being
all right when you meet yourself coming or going.
I've got a bee talking soft zeros near
the tree outside my window. I've got an eye

that can look right through. I've got a soul
full of salt like an olive. I've got a cleaning woman
who comes and touches all my things. Who raises them up
and sets them down. I've got an idea they love her

not me. I've got an idea each girl dumb like the spring thinks
she's the first and only. I've got a notion to sit here
all day and get the blues about the light
and how it will feel in ten years. I don't know why.

Sometimes the past walks right through me like an old boyfriend.
Sometimes the past like an old boyfriend walks
through me. I don't know if I say goodbye
or hello or drink coffee. If I answer

its question or get distracted hearing
my mother and father come in late
and drop their coats. It's spring '60.
Their dark feet swim near my door and their voices

hook on the taut line of whispers. I've got a line
on those whispers. I've got them
hushing each other, my mother and father,
coming in strong and late. They're saying

words low as wounds given under water, words
without lights on and I'm bursting to tell them
hushing each other, my mother and father,
I'm awake, still awake. Wide awake.

To a Girl Writing Her Father's Death

Sometimes the lake water writes and writes and gets
no answer. You tell me, It was just October.
That is good. His voice was full of love and laughter. Not
so good. Full of copper, jacks-of-diamonds, cubes
of honey, I could believe. But I did not know
your father. The moment when the cable snapped from
the boat has, however, its drama. Yet is not
enough. Try to understand the need out here for
gestures, wind, raw sound. Was it a spasm
of sex in the motor, light shingling
his black hair as the boat spun
on its wide iris down? Were you standing?
I know this must be painful, standing
at the edge of your white page with someone
gone under. You were sixteen and he called you
Princess, though it is a cliché to be
called Princess. And to be sixteen. Yet
I have looked at you and you are not now
much older. You could wear tiaras,
your blonde waves pure as the back
of the knee. Though you wear your carrot rouge
in clumsy circles, which makes me
love you. I have not lost a father
except in dreams. But each one has left
my mouth open. Speak. Make holy
detail. Let the water bead over you like cold
eyeballs. Let in the scream and the lining of the scream
and the prismic figure eights of oil
made on the wake—and forgive me
for asking. You have to think of the world
which gave and took your father.
The world which asks for him now.
There's no sense writing poems unless
you see the mob: We who gather for the red
pulse of every ambulance, we who crowd
lifeguards kissing the still blue lips of children
on the beach, and murmur who
and how, hungry for every morsel
of this life that is not ours, not really. Not
for long. But for the asking.

The Winged Eye

When I go to hell they weigh my heart.
The walls are painted with the lacquer
gaze of jilted brides. I wonder why I am here.

The devil comes, soft and cloven like a burnt cake.
He opens his manual.
It is called *How To Interpret Your Dreams*.
We sit in the garden where lips

purse in the snapdragons. A chicken
lands on his arm leaving its claw
print in his skin like creases in the cardboard
seal of a cereal box

pressed beneath a thumb.
When he reads he moves his mouth.
When he looks up he asks me if I remember
the world with swans. He

misses them most. My eye,
he says, has wings. He reminds me of
an old boyfriend who told me the greatest
men, the greatest minds in the world have

believed in God. It was much
like this. We were leaning by the river, sweet
helixes of light unhinging in
the current, and I was waiting for

a kiss. Not philosophy. And not
the devil's pining.

Love, Scissor, Stone

In April, he had forgotten where I was.
He was thinking of the stars and the police
badges deflecting little signals
where the night went down over my body
on the riverbed road. When I came back

from the dead, he was angry. It was past
midnight. He had already been rehearsing
his behavior at the inquest, already
prepared the emptiness, scoured and transparent
as a guest wing in our house. Moths

had opened a place in their burning books
for me as the headlights threw
the west wall up and its window—the one
we'd bricked and plastered over from
the inside to block the morning

scissor light. The cat clouded
two perfect jades as I came in, and the vase
was there, right there on the table,
a thickening in the water and a loose
wand of stock

had snowed around it where I sometimes
left a coffee cup, a note. I had risen
and was walking toward a place to leave
my shoes. He was in the half-light.
Or it was the sawed shadow

of that door. Once, he had wanted me
alive. We had slept in the corridors of hot
Italian trains all night, bread
in our suitcases and one-shot bottles
of brandy. But now

it was only spring. Some year. And his eyes
came flat at me, asked me where
the hell I was. I was

without a word for once, and turned

down the hallway to the room of shoes,
and ashtrays, and cool cups, where I
sometimes wrap that word
around a stone.
And though I could lie

I do not. Though I could say in love
when there's not the light place there's
the buried place, that when he fell asleep
the house was breath
dovetailing breath,

I am not sure
I could believe it. There is, after all,
a life to live, not speaking, through dinner,

at twilight. I know no man or woman
plans this. It seems always
to happen suddenly, as if we've been
sleeping. Then awakened. And the smell of citrus
is curded in the night air, sour

and too sweet. But we bear it.
Because it's here. It's where
the hell we are.

Monsoon

The heaviness of twilight at noon. Stillness
like a thug in the wings. The sky thinks
over glass. A man stares at the telephone.
There is the moment that waiting becomes
luminous, the roundness of the air visible
as he had always guessed. He hangs in the dome
with a few green leaves. Then darkness

cinches the house up in its sack.
And you know how people think of things once
inside. Sometimes he thinks of dialing the number
that used to bring his mother's voice. Would it
ring, would it reach a woman with flour
like moon seas on her apron, string
around her finger. A reminder.
Perhaps it is connected

to the voice that says I'm sorry.
To the man who is passing the booth.
Perhaps he would interrupt a robbery or love.

The cloud smashes open like fruit.
The ozone of junipers rinsed in gin.
He thinks when the dead die, children go in
and lift the lids of the music boxes
in their rooms. They discover how jewels are places
lonelier than darkness. The rain better

than a thousand mothers.

My Husband's Bride

The past begins to move at night.
A white peony too open from the heat
catches a soft light in its hackles
a room away from where the body, lost
from sleep like the amorous stranger,
the mental America, sits
with a little vodka turning
the stares of guests
in the wedding album. I hear
another year rustle by like the night's
one car. I put my hand through
the bed's blind side.
He is with her again. The bride
smiling where her shadow's thrown
a black water she could walk.
It's a day like spring in January,
a bloom pinned to the chest
where the body's grown back
over its life. All around our house
couples have begun to die
of a mysterious unhappiness.
Their supper tables have thinned
to wire. Their touch like jars
where a little doubt flutters.
They have disproved equation
after equation that a woman
and a man traveling time can get out
young again and promise everything.
But it is not hers now.
The bride's face is like the delicate
print of the face of my thumb,
the part of me I have lost
but lost to him.

Adam

Crushed the first time
in the heavy hand
of mud, he hung
upside-down among the nurse
stars, and ached

like the last
plum of that first summer.
He wanted the Angel of Morphine,
the mouth open
on the void. Each day, yes,

was forever. Heaven
held his leg by a hook.
He found he was subject
to Laws. Principles.

They took his water
in bags. They brought him
flowers. He could see light
condense to touch
the throat of the vase.
The nothings
I would use to turn him, head

over heel, in the next life.
But there, in desire's swoon
he watched small cattle throb
the earth, and the wrists
of the rivers.
Then the blackout.

I see it in his eyes
when he walks past me, the flash
of a pin in his hip: The dream
of rabbits hanging in the trees,
the tufts of the body,
and the bone

purple, jutting
from the paradise
of the lost.

Satan's Box

When I come in late, the devil is up
writing his sonnet. He's drinking jasmine
tea. In search of a word he lifts the top
from his Russian box lined with velvet where
an io moth is spinning on a pin.
He sets aside

a child's one-eyed bear,
my mother's cloth tomato pincushion,
my father walking, blue button, black pen,
all the things I will never see again.

I take advantage of the commotion,
peer over his shoulder where the i's are
dotted with Pentecostal hearts. It starts:
Remembrance is a fire in a drawer, ends:
Your house will melt on hinges like a star.

In the Middle of Things, Begin

Bees rode the scalloped air of the garden.
The table, glazed bowls set for the afternoon meal,
trembled. A woman flashed in the archway
clutching her jewel box and her infant,
shoving them into a cart. The sleep was over.

I am near the mountain when you wake me,
the darkness ancient as the tongue
in a stone. You had slept a few hard hours
and then did not know where you were.
Small room on the Italian coast, it is strange
to us. I hear you touch things. I put up

my hand. I say *here, here.* We still
love each other. But this was years ago.
In the morning, we wander the ruins
of Pompeii, rooms cracked by golden
broom flowers, dry mosaic of a pool where
blind boy Cupid stands, the limed

jet in his loins. We step inside
the tepidarium, pale corruptions of pipe
and wall, and circle slowly the people
of ash, molded to their moment behind
the glass. Cocooned so perfectly
in the postures of death, their bodies

tire us, even the dog's legs curled
to the tickle of stillness, torso
torqued almost playfully. We forget
it was the cloud they died from, not
the burning, not the fire. But the gray world.
Woman lying with her knees drawn up, cheek
resting on her hands. Man with his head

turned, hands flat, arms bent like a mantis
as if to push away the kiss of earth.
I am remembering them now in the middle
of things, like the married in their
separate, fitful sleep. Suffocation

and climax: Same slow drag of the mouth. Same gouged bread of the face.

The Ecstasy

As if bone spilled
down the stairway of a long night
her marble dress unfolded the seven
sevens of light. We had come
to see the saint. And on a weekday,
only a few of the penitent
in the back pews kneeled, old women
with the blue of sin already
seeing through their hands. It was the arrow
through the heart, the hundred butterflies pinned

by one pin—the moment that was always
woman in the stone. I'd come with the girl who saved
her butter from lunch to eat later on the train,
who talked to Jesus in her sleep. She
was twenty-five and no man had ever loved her, ever
would. She stood transfixed as if the place
is white, where joy is, and then began
to giggle, pointing

low where a skeleton lay in gold
and lilac vestments behind the glass. Its hair
the dull of hemp against the pillow. "Look,"
she said. "Look at the doll." I saw the face
of the dead, face where the devil's bear had sucked
all the honey from the comb.

Yet as this was, after all, a church, and we
were strangers, and this was Italy, bright summer,
I touched the girl, felt the quiver of her shoulder
and it almost took
like a laughter from the next world
or that sadness in sex
until she turned, one iris more astonished
than the other, as if the right eye were always
far away: An age, another country, and like
the blue that is a pomegranate in its dreams.

Leda

I wanted to be like blindness in the river.

That morning the tight hum of cicadas
snapped into a fine silence. I cut
my finger on a reed, sucked
the little salt of myself as I let
the garment fall. *Something in the air,*

I might have said, as old men before
a fire, a battle. I walked the mouth
of river mud, thick lips of those Nubian
boys in sleep, then turned suddenly half
expecting their wild eyes and giggles.
I had a stone. But there was only the flat

wineskin of my shadow, and one cloud
beating with light which followed me,
my hips threaded with water
as I floated back, my skull light
in the bell pull of my hair.

When the first feather struck
I remembered the slave girl's stillborn,
its melded hand, its hole for nose,
its sealed eyes. We buried him shallow
in a grove of aleppos. This
is not the god's story—it is mine.
It is not straight. It is how the swan

warped my shape in his, like the second
ring of water the first. He moved
like a way, not a thing: All
hypothetical particles, shuddering
W's and Z's. And it was breath first
I fought for through the creature's weight
heavy with the odor of musk, of cumin.
My nails sank into the tender edge
of thunder. Rabid snow. He shoved
his hard comb into my hair, and wasted

me with light. I am the leper whose heart
falls out first. But when I rose,

at last, from the river
in the thousand drops of my skin
I was boiling. I was a woman . . .

I do not want to be one with anything.

The Lives of the Poets

The palms rustled like torch rags
where the sky blew out. There was a half-moon.
Behind us the old hotels clung
to the strand of beach only by the nerve
of their neon, a blue, a concentrating pink.
Out there, ocean brooded like a magnet.
The air was good like chains.
It was simple: We could step off
America itself. Someone

stashed a cigarette in the sand.
And the night came after it. Bloomed
from our eyes. When we passed the breakwall
there was an old woman there,
dress hiked up on her plump knee, face
tilted in the stiff moon of her hair. And
the old man, standing, crushed
into her with the kind of kiss
that shamed us by its randy glory

and resurrected us in hunger.
When we stood later letting the waves
salt our ankles, just far out enough
to feel where the world goes soft,
the length of the shore was only shadow,
breeze hummed with the odor of fish.
Two of the men stripped down and swam out.
The women waded, torn. My mind

was the nude glistening out of this—
all we wanted of darkness
was for the wanting not to leave us,
the burnt eternal
pawing us with its last warm breath.
And it was almost midnight
when we took the last good look,
turned into the streets saying
we should all write
a poem about this, waiters lit

in the windows of hotel kitchens,
some traffic, and the drugstore's bricks
spray-painted with Spanish gang names and

that one American and primal word.
It was red as a thing split open.
A valentine. And we paused, waiting
at the corner as if this were no place
to end, remembering how empty
sweater sleeves draped her shoulders,
how her ankles locked and lifted
and he buried his face in her neck.
And he held her, sagging and all,
the black gulf behind them going all the way—

In the Badlands of Desire

If there is the statue of a saint
whose toes are worn smooth from old women
kissing, if there is an animal whose name
is sleep, if there is a hill
whose bones are broken, I
will remember me in the next life.

If there is an onion with the hundred
smaller and smaller faces
of wet light, if there is a mirror
whose shoulders drift
the museum of shoulders,

there is a spider like a dud star
which catches the empire
from table leg to corner, if there are communists
and useless lingerie, and rubies
snatched at night from jewelers' windows,
I will be the butcher's white

paper, the hook raving in frost.
If there is a tongue still moving
toward its mother silence, mint still breaking
its unimaginable green fist
through old aqueducts where the drunk

meet to be lonely and violet
as nets sieving the shine of nothing,
if there is a plaza in a town
where the stones break out
like hives in the plaster, and pigeons
blow their cool oboes of love,

I will be the look given to a door
when it closes by itself. After
it closes, wondering
was it some hand, some wind. And if it is painted
blue, like the faded crepe of old hours, if

a wolf bares its teeth to its tail
on the doorstep, there will be a hard winter,
a demon spring.

Never be the Horse (1999)

My Bomb

Better than a dream, it left gargantuan
roses in the Japanese garden, and the rabbits
heavy as children. We would crouch
in the classroom beneath our desks
and concentrate on being small, study
the whitecaps of our knees. Once

we went below the library,
the dark shelves stacked with cans
of creamed corn, green beans, mandarin oranges
we'd eat like the dead for five years
and rise again. Thus,

I learned the catechism: proton, electron,
neutron. I learned to contemplate
the Invisible. I went to sleep

in the fire-cloud folding like the brain
and dreamt about the power of my bomb,
girls flashing to the sidewalks, cities
filigreed, the bird-cinders,
light bright as the mirror on the shoe of God

and afterward, pink as phoenixes,
the American Beauties pressing their
mammoth lips to the charge of the sky.
This is how I loved the earth

with my life. With the pure nuclei of
my matter. How it fell into my hands.
Better than desire,
my bomb lit the face of my own

twentieth century. I had it
so no one could use it. I would have more
so no one could have enough.

Since I Have Lived

Since I have lived in the desert all summer I've learned
the sound closest to water is the slush of the rabbit
through the dead blossoms beneath the oleander.
Next to this, paper. Next,
cars.

I am thinking of the black tongue of the king snake near the shed.
Also the black tongue of your cancered mother—

All the nurses gave us
was a small sponge on a stick
to swab her lips. And finally nothing to do
but tell her, tell her it was all right.

We were devils and angels.
We were wrong, but wrong in the face of helplessness is right.
To do the only thing. And since I have lived

with you, the newly-dead's son. The long-dead's, the
childhood's cut rope. The sound of your sleep is like

sipping the house. The house is dry, dry
and the shortest night of the year is coming
and I'll sleep all morning and I'll take

time and put its one leg in one leg of my pants
and my leg in the other. I'll be alive,
since rising at last is what the living do—

Outside, all down the dry wash rocks spark.
A bird breaks out like a buoyant door.

Which cracks wide my head. Good,
since the ratio of land to water is changing,

and candelabras to fish. Such is wishing, my desert, such
is willing, that for the moment
everything we do metes out
justice. As when the nurse didn't come

my father told me how to insert the catheter
in him, and when he asked
did it embarrass me I said no it did not
embarrass me. For I was at last
given the instruction, given the task to do,
the words to follow, the devil to pay.

The sound of my breath the sound of an upside down cup.

A Day Passes Through the Medium of Identity

The pine like the wet proof
rising from twilight
does not give away
what century this is. Dusk
cools to a plum of nitrogen.
The birds spread their empire
of melancholic wit. In this,
I could be St. Augustine, Aurelius,
or my own lost grandmother
as a girl humming by the window.

At a universal point
the birds' ecstatic industry
shuts down. I have been wondering
about this for days. Wondering if
we are in the same life—
or if I should curse the house
bringing me such truths. The truth is

I once wrote an elegy for Keats,
having stood in the window of his house,
a museum on the Piazza di Spagna.
There was a lock of his hair
you were not allowed to touch—
the color of balsa or summer
grass. The death mask

lay on the table by his bed.
The window overlooked a cloud
of potted hydrangeas on the steps.
But if you did not look down,
straight out there was only a pure
level of blue, an absolute box
of sky, the kind of view ascribed

to the dead. I told my friend I did not
feel his spirit. And in the very room where . . .

He could have been the *lamia*
or even a Roman street thief
when he lay in his sick bed and

watched the chalky hour before
morning. The fever was erotic.
The nightingale did not love him.
Its short elliptical breaths
were the effort to raise
his root once, imagining

fat madonnas blowing on
their breakfast fires and air
glassing at the fringe—
a seat off the spirit
which could be Rafaello, or Autumn,
or Christ: The seed of a man
hotter and briefer
than the dark bitch of poetry.

Hound and Leper

The madwoman in gloves
has let her hand blow open
through soily eyelets, and points
one finger at me across the street.
You're so ugly, she yells.
And in the tinny sunlight I glance
behind me hoping to see
the grotesque. *Where'd you get*
such an ugly face?
She approaches, her blue socks
in rings and a man's shoe
mouthing open at the toe.
I walk on straight and slowly
like my loved ones told me . . .

She shakes her fist as I pass.
A pigeon is whining in the palm tree
and some house with a passion vine
tangles to my left. Will she
follow me, my accuser:
Hash-haired, malty-breathed, eyes of
aluminum and string. At the bridge,
she passes under and I
over the hard crease and quartz,
fossil print of the river
whose mirror has walked. She's seen it,
the disfigurement of dream,
hound and leper in my face—
how flesh is always on
the scent of something, and the marrowy
suck of my eye is creating
symbiosis: Hunger and denial.

It is the one who does not love you
whom you finally believe. Tonight in that
drift before sleep, her voice
is his. On the ceiling, Eros
rides Psyche. I sleep disguised
as myself, my derelict.
Where'd you get that mouth? Christ.
Her eyes hidden behind her hand,
midstreet. My no one.

My confessor. My lips are red iron.
I can't bear their secret.
I'd stuff them with dynamite
and run. Straight home,
like my loved ones said.

I Have Set My Heart on the Sparrow

It is as if one set out to love
one of the sparrows flying past and
behold, it has vanished . . .
　　　　　　　—Marcus Aurelius

One world is always beginning.
The cows meet like the burdens of sleep
in a field, each one
bearing a white part a black part
of the map. I snow

right there, they hardly notice
interference—memory—
They mean to freeze with
their eyes set longingly
on the farmhouse,

eyes like mud trying
to say *love*. Eyes like cows
loving a house, or deciding
smoke from the chimney.

Smoke begins in the belly.
Mother and Father, you are there.
There, this time, without me.
I can't begin—

All night I listened to one bird
from my bed, after it had rained.
I said, Imagine there is nothing
to the world but you and the bird—
this one throaty waterfaller, this
small surge, this diamond-chipper. Bird.
It sings. You listen.
It can't conceive of you. You listen.
One bubble in the darkness—

That's where I fell
asleep. Where a language
I know only as a language went on
alone. The spilled connection . . .

It's the life again where God
says I can only use three details:
I arrange and I arrange.
I want to be able to say farewell.
I was told once what birds mean:

Their calling is only
"I'm a lark," "I'm a wren,"
"I'm a starling, starling, starling."
"This is my territory."

I dream my first memory. House,
I tell the cows
I will love that bird forever.

Swallower

Open the cupboard, cherries rounded up in the darkness.
Sometimes the childhood mystery of the old woman's room.
Its scent bulging out from the polished wooden things,
   from the laciness over which the mirror threw
   back the room, scent wormholing

personal galaxy to personal galaxy. Space is the problem,
the whole
   weep of it. Most of the time. The cherries
themselves, swallowers. All that inked-up redness.
As if the eye-mouth-nostril angel of orifices was
   the only guardian, only

loop into good time. Now

the self is a hundred vigils.
Some of them over bowls and silent bureaus,
some of them over blood-relations, over
that moon over *is this the right bus.*
Then.

Once. I was struck sick while climbing a hill—all
I looked for was a place to heave myself, kneel
and quiver. Even as I approached the feverish
   patinations of my wing-split I knew the trees
   flowering east were tasseling

sheer memory. Its marriages I hate.
The cherries take you
somewhere in you that's out of order: China

dogs lustery on the sill, fleur-de-lised
wallpaper, the rouged-up faces of hand-tinted photographs.
Each face a pulp tightened around a single incident.
How shall I leave the room when I die?

Outside my house the fence wood swells after
rain, the air heavy as fruit. The error is in the equation,
fragrance was a gate upon the heart,
yet only one
   the responsible object.

The Book of Hens

The wasp wants to be a bell.
This is what I learn in June. I add it
to the things I have confirmed
this year: I am missing.

Here the pomegranate tree has all
blossoms on hold like my dream head—
My mother and father are just married.
My husband and I are just meeting.
He is born.
I am seven, cradling my red dog
for the first time.

I'm the clock with twenty hands.
I am stuck between the past—

Add to this the manuscript I opened
in my studious sleep. I got no further
than the table of contents, titles
my eye ran down:
The Hen Myself
The Rider in the Hen
The Belgian Hen's Monologue to the Tree
I Am the Hen
Hens Eating at Dusk

The heart wants to be—
anything in it.

The Painted Adam

After the first bite of guilt,
after the dazzling horizon of nakedness
when she was bathing, he saw the skins
laid on the boulder, their fringe,
the downy tips of quail feathers,
folds in the lambskin she tied across
her breasts. He took them to heart
and bound himself, confined the flat-
haloed nipples, caught hairs in the knot.
Feathers flew at his arms and ribs as he
juiced the childish pomegranate against rock,
stained his lips, opened her horn of eyepaint,
fingered the ball-lightning of his lids. It was
like holding shocked wood doves before
their necks snapped. How could he be calm?
He began to pulse as if the woman-bone
buried in him rose, this bitch resurrection
come at last: His new aura, his
plumage, his torchy glances dithering
the lagoon through the red
drag of jasmine, his reflection blinking
back its wounds of earring until his hips
swayed and he danced dressed as Want You,
this masquerade, the flesh
twirled to take beauty
from behind, hosanna, to multiply
a ravishment of one.

Whitman's Confession: In the Cleft of Eternity

. . . look for me under your bootsoles.

What happened was my last breath fell back
on me like pins, the Ultimates—
and my hand slushed through
my chest into stars: None of you
mattered anymore, my nipples pointing off
the sawgrass and your faces all
dooryard. I did not wait for you long.
When the body was gone, there was not even perfume.
There was a suck

like a choir about to and then not. I
tell you of the kosmos, vast puke
and scintillation. We do not go anywhere.
And when my eye studied
the catechism of the image, it went: Worm,
nest, bridge, reflection, stripe rolling over
into worm. What happened was they

struck me with the bomb of the Buddha,
all the multitudes from the top of my head and from
the ribs' shoelace. I withered firsthand, text,
translation, emanation, ink, and rag
into the cud of the Milky Way, thrush-
bone and mule-bone
wheeling in the dander-fields and through
the clean bowels of Orion
turning me over the blue straight-

hairs of the diamond. *Is this then a touch?*
What happened is I lost the animal of my likeness,
Earth of fur—
Earth of legitimate odors and of nights arm-in-arm.
I no longer know who set the woman on that road
or how her face can shape to what is missing.
I no longer know that the clasp of a man
is the cuttle of my vibrations.
Or that the lapidary of distances is memory—

Or that milk is cold.
You will not find me in any energy,
the tender, the gross, the metastasized, the skittish,
the thrilling, the angelic. I hit the Void
running, and it was easy to betray you.
I could not wait for you. The poem
was the god who only yearned
to fuck alone.

Once a Shoot of Heaven

Even when you see through the lies, the lies they
fed you as a child, you
still believe some of it, still, when you drift
from thinking. When the air's true and simple
like a sheet you've laundered for as long

as you can remember, and your mother before you. There was an end,
and a beginning, and love, and wrong and right and
someone who loved the world and someone who did not
and someone who made the moon and the moon that just was.
Always.

Now there's a white disappearing brow at the edge of September,
usual stars.
        A siren sets off a dog.
        A car radio flies down the road.
        In between, the acacias tick, tick in a lightness not yet wind.

        The early bird is asleep.
        The world still isn't safe for democracy.

There was a mother and a father and a child and an hour
and exactly so many minutes, and left and right,
and people who ascended like doves and people
who slept in the earth, and apples that could make you strong
and sugar that could make you weak, and people who burned.

And tonight you still talk to someone who is not there, not
        yourself—crazy promises, little pleas, momentary

thanksgivings. This no one who has never been there
is like the cat who only went away they said

to live and raise a family in the Christenson's barn. So there was
the one who went on living forever and the one you realized
could not live forever.

Here there's the sound of a neighbor dragging his trash cans
down the driveway to the curb. No one on this street sleeps.

The crickets are poor not lucky.
The ear might as well be gold.

With a Ravenous Spike

I know that city coyote
will take the moon in his teeth tonight,
it's so thin, low,
a pith between darkness and fruit.
Sometimes between the houses
in the last hour still safe from dawn,
an animal scuttle breaks out—snarls,
then the high-pitched yips quick as if greased
from fear. The cat slips through the drapes to the window,
crouches, all hackle. A sheer pleat
rumples against her. How far we've come.
I'm listening as something scuffs away, rattling
the oleander, my past life, ancient Greek life—
not a shepherd, just another girl who stayed awake.
Still, my moods of eternity are brief.
I'll find the torn jackrabbit in the morning.
Coyote, I've heard you come and depart,
even the week I had fever. My ears burned
as if someone secretly desired me, but who
I'd never guess. In my childhood fevers it was
death with cool hands, death who'd singled me out
and I'd lie in my own dewy beatitude,
a hamstrung ache, listening to cars, voices, distant
mowing, oh, they'd miss me. But now I'm older,
now I'm well and the world that goes on around me is
the first one, the one I could only enter
on four legs, with a keen nose, with a ravenous
spike of hunger in my skull. I know that
city coyote has slunk back up the mountain
stinking of rabbit, moon spittle in the rock hollows,
and is satisfied, done with his purpose. Done
with Plato. With Rousseau. With Cartesian nonsense.
He has eaten, enough. He is am.
There is no light yet; a new mint of quiet comes.
Then a three-minute scumble of dream:
Roads again, always roads I've missed
the turn for, roads I'm taking straight up
like the backward film of a waterfall, smack
into waking. Jesus

Christ, the second life no more
whole than the first. If I were let out now like a cat
under the chariots and necklaces and
ladles of the stars—under the bear and swan—
to brush my jowls against some cool nursemaidy flower,
I'd know What For. The moon, my Lapland.
I'd know that city coyote as death, testicled
and hairy, one rung above me in the hierarchy
of death as, below me, the rung of rabbit-death, then
lizard-death, down into beetle-death
and the last step off snail-death into
amoebic void. But in this body's slow distinction
to blues, this hour, the east coming out like a scarf
on a balcony, there's nothing but parity—
cars passing childhood and passing now
on the highway, this hunter's hour—a parity of coolness
and hand, dream and ear. Coyote, I return
to my only true subject in light
of desert autumn; no amount of road or house
or urban sprawling drives me out. Though long-winged
memory pursues me: The chick responds to the shadow
of a hawk even before it's out of the shell. And in my bed,
the fever's passing made me wonder if daily a secret combustible
need makes a man quieter, more polite, more
carefully correct, lest he flame—
We are what eats us, Coyote.
The dog-star's fading and the only woman-star
I can name is a burning princess once
fed to the jaws of a serpent.
A story before you sleep. From that dark cave
poked in the mountain, the city is only haze, glint.
The day begins with what
we've left behind. Oh, slowly, I get to my eyes,
face, mouth, shirt, stunned kitchen.
The ground is mantled pink. Quail are walking.
How—do we come back to this
world without iron bands around our hearts
without moon dripping from our teeth, blood
matted in our hair and the one-below-us-in-death
deep in our belly? Oh, I know that sour coyote

would taste worse than spinach and pine pitch,
bitter as the Passover radish. Wafer on Passion Sunday.
But I, like the golden chicken,
butter with cinnamon, rich as the drowned
housefly sipped with the wine.

Never Be the Horse

Night on night a horse stood in the hull
crossing an ocean.
It tried to dream on the smell of damp oatseed
its former country, the spongy field
and the clop of a hoof. Later
came winds and a blanket
thrown and a bearded rider swung up
clicking his tongue there in the dark ark's hold.
O they could see dirt roads by the hundreds
vaulted with tamarisks,
the early springs, the breath-apples of winters.
But where were they going—
two sips wobbled in a huge goblet, pitched
and yawed, the constant paradiddle of rain,
doves shitting the rafters. The rider said a voice
had promised on the other side of water
was a green prairie, horizon snug as a rib.
And the horse thought, Never be the horse God talks to.
The waves reached a gallop just
beneath them, reached the horizon and thinned
to sweat, and still
the horse slept upright in the ripe blackness.
Or so they assumed,
the deck passengers, terns, cherubim, archangels, etc.
Months later, a rock rose and then low furzy branches.
Then in each ankle a bell clapped for the mud.

Lucifer's Crown

1

He dreamt of an apple big as a house,
of a snake smooth as tears. He dreamt a mine
opened in his pillow, plutonium
crouched inside the pitchblende, an opal
in the bowels. Before, all his dreams had been
of falling—that sexual vertigo—
of windflowers between his ears and his
belly dropping out like a wine jug through
a wet paper sack. He was simple as
a man who in his loneliness believed
everything in a different room
of his heart, a master politician
for these, the troubled times which now were just
beginning, now that God had left his bed.

2

Beginning now that God had left his bed,
he put on a beard of glittered nightsweat,
the musk of the oryx, iridescent
pigeon-ring, stockings of the panther, yet
it was no use—each form an extension
of his discontent, until the dream wound
back to him and he put on the slick tongue—
until his body was a mind turning
into itself, its wonder-twister, its
who am I, its why, its wanting over
and over, its loopy memory . . . Now
snuffed of every grace but talk of it,
the beginning was the word and the word was
flesh, flesh became the world and he was it.

3

Flesh, flesh became the world and he was it:
The garden odors were like his staircase
fallen, clove on jasmine, on shaved cedar,
on punk loams, on mineral gladness. So
he descended. In her depth, the woman
was alone. The rake dropped behind her. He
tried to say something with leaves. Then he swirled
up and kissed her. It wasn't that he was
beautiful and brilliant, a nova of
mothers-of-pearl, but that she could smell on
his breath, already, the death camps, little
incident in Armenia, slave ships,
Prague Spring, and she loved his small mouth full of
gossamer gibber, that heavenly French.

4

Gossamer gibber, that heavenly French
spinning endlessly from the spider sac
between his teeth, swan-necked syllables, quenched
consonants and vowels, round Cadillacs
of sound, his whisper's plush upholstery
where her ear curled up, morphemic mysteries
with seven veils and seven gold lit wicks
in oil behind them, *burnt lark, burnt heart,* she
began to lip-read him like fire, mimic
light lost, light lost—poor blackballed angel, he
waved and said Let there be, and there was not.
There was evening, and he could not rest
his voice, still his quick fricatives, stop
the one thing that made him more than a beast.

5

The one thing that made him more than a beast,
less than a star, let him charge the holy

atmosphere unnoticed except that birds
would freeze a moment and moths would dash him.
And less than a newborn bomb let him drop
at her feet and roll, this smart of matter
known as the Evil One, Prince, Fiend, Old Scratch.
The one thing was he could articulate
his silence, the way a homesickness must
sound the past or a dark lust ventriloquize
the present. More than a lover, less than
a friend, he sweet-nothinged her: *Here we are,*
oh, Eve-bird, this our human fate, to be
in paradise longing for paradise.

6

In paradise, longing for paradise,
each leaf loved its pointed face on the calm
water and fell for it. Each grape in its
cluster loved its shadow on the other.
Each thing stood its tiny doll on its head
in the dark of his eye and his reason
righted it. Thus he practiced like the world
small tricks to order his memory. But
each time he succeeded, chaos increased;
each epiphany used more fuel than
it gave. For two lights must go out for one
to go on in memory, and the mind
in desiring undress down to its horns,
lock with hunger, knock its back to earth.

7

Lock with hunger, knock its back to earth,
it was no angel glorious like he,
but it would do—the demon's demon, yes,
the spitting in his own image. Drown it.

Mourn it. Sex it. The soul, apoplectic
blossom. How beauty would craze him who could
not hold it, though the mere sight of the moon
would nearly crack his loins. Smother it, nail
hit on his own head: He was the woman
inside the woman, man inside the man,
the blackbird alive in the pie. Eat it.
Sleep. Simple as a child at night who dreams
it's light, he was light. Fallen. Rockabyed.
And rolled back the apple of his big eye.

Retro Lullaby

Sometimes I carry the smell of moist hay from my childhood.
      And sometimes I put down this burden, never
      without its consent. Long have I

known memory and willingness to be one fold,
      though I find it difficult to talk to my childhood
      since I had the flying dream—my robes

      bubbled over the desert—
And now all I have is a postcard of a little stranger.
If I drop the card in the hay-smell,

her ear will plump up like a dried apricot in wine.
And her stupid white hands will come up like two
      white pages from the bottom of a lake

And I'll coo, It's ok, you can be my baby.
      My part.

I can never remember the whole day.

After all, my sister said I was a strange child, an automaton.
My mother said if they talked idly in February
      of going somewhere in June, I'd wake in June,
my suitcase packed.

Terrible she said to have a child who never forgot a thing.

But now, of course, I've slipped
      my mind forever in some infeasible way, flown

stiff as a toy in my dream altitude and I remember
wondering even in my elation if I'd drop
      suddenly and if I did

I don't remember. But if I did, I'd say,
      It's ok, you can be my angel. You can be
      my human kite.

At any time, we might give in. Just a knuckle of us,
      or a cheek. Because the
      ferment of the hayfield unpacks on the side of a road
      and one second

gets the Gone going again, her little hairs stand up.

And childhood stinks big in our lives as death.
And in between is willingness—her tongue comes out
      speaking its *motherese*—

All right. You can be my lake, my June, my hay-fish.
      Be my keen hound. My. Love of My Life.

The Tongue of the Sphinx

—for Rick Noguchi

What's the difference
between graverobbing and poetry?

It doesn't matter how you found it
but that you dragged the old
porcelain commode to the middle of your yard,
shining, useless, to your back window,
In the afternoon, you said, it looks friendly,
But at night it's the Blue Morpho, a stare
into the terror of objects.
I said, Some night watch who comes
and sits there:

The grocer from childhood, the ancestor,
the loved one's ignominious death—
I meant this for you, but I was haunted,
and what the moon lit was that white
open, your absurd muse. And your
most private. Wasn't it Stevens who said
resist

the pressure of reality? Wasn't it Freud
who said all children
believe their shit is precious? Think

what relief is there for our lives,
for the lives of those who love us
when we are always watching—
as if otherwise their nakedness
would go to waste. I want you to hear
my confession: I saw my father stricken
and wrote it down. I saw my husband's
darkness and I wrote it down. I saw
his father leaned against the bathtub
with his soiled trousers undone, weeping
and his wife gone and his house sold

and the nasturtiums they planted still blooming
and I wrote it down.

What's the proper punishment
for stealing a life—a hand   two hands
a hand and a foot?

Look, tonight,
who is out there. Someone who wants only
some time to read, some time alone—
someone I love,
someone whose eye is like the burn-ring
in the gold poppy . . .

Use him, use him if you can.

For what is the difference
between thievery and love?

Money

It is wrong to stay here and talk forever, the sack of thunder
over the black mountains still cinched, a shudder

and a batting of violet. The late monsoon wanders, nods off.
The nights clear and the stars know where to cut.
I have not moved. The voice wheedles out of its smallness
fondling each pitch, up

against the thigh of some death. Who can understand
the misery of the finch—this one

summer just ebbing has been its whole year,
the first coolness, the first mother-death, time's so
bird-fast.

And I, I who was born with a fascinated tongue,
sit bare-kneed in the eclipse. The moon

coppers until its cradle cap—so white—slips back
to be the strange chip Mongolia must see,
its people just rising—that mirror hour

fainting into frank blueness. Knowing two things at
one time is the endless money of the distance,

and the dream of a perfect match
for your mouth, your nature, your breeding season,
is your

crush on the down of night, the fall
coming. I wish

to be hunted and found, and found, shot, and
shot, rocked with grief and bandaged, and bandaged,

given time.

Being Pharaoh

My grandmother turned into an old man,
deaf, with a hairy chin. It is August,

the damp panting of nights—I am
gradually building my own underworld

not just with prospective grief but
wires to hold up the asphodels.

Into it, a whole migration of shapes
skinned by light, pears gone

flat, and cars, and shadow like a floored heart.
They're the file of a river

and the Greeks had a river, the Romans.
The Egyptians who civilized the dead.

Tonight I am sick of every man
and his past. And the past is tired of his

request that it love him. I am trying
to make my bed. I am trying to keep

an angel from cracking my hip. The moon's
sleeve is flipped back in a drawer . . .

Thrush, you little singing spade—
I'm an unforgivably domestic mourner

and I might sleep through someone's
late supper, or hunger—just think how

oblivious he will be. While I am in
the dark rustling my own inventory:

Each time we fall out of love we
say it wasn't really love at all as if

landing, a plane would say *no, not
actual sky*. While I am in the dark

getting fit for an afterlife. Admit
we never know the difference, like the woman

who stands up in the cinema and becomes
the black keyhole we peer into. I am

trying to keep her head down. So long
even her mother and mother's mother

turn blue. I am trying to keep
the ancestors out of the bedroom

so I can conceive a new face and new
arms, the feather trees across

the river, the curious shore dog.
Keep the distance simple like the top

deck of the parking garage from which
we can see the hospital. The present

may bond to any molecule, future
or past: My parents were kissing

while someone dragged the body past
the doorway, bag zipped to the chin

on the gurney, the head wound in white gauzes.
My father had taken off his mask, still

hissing oxygen, and mother was bent.
Of all the things I've seen it was

old love that kept them from seeing.
Beautiful discretion, what moment will you

save from me? This should have been
a dream, something to wake from

but I never do. I am trying.
I will be pharaoh yet—

sealed with tiny boats and slavish
figurines. I am sick of every face

floating a sex by itself. Take in
this lampshade and these

curtains. Objects are memory.
As a child, I pictured the soul as a glass

wing, fluted, gelatinous, detached
as my voice underwater. I made it up

a body—a paperweight—no snow
in the water, no water under the earth,

no music ever again in my hair, after
my hair. The dead will point to it,

What was the name for this, point to my hand,
What was the name for this? One life

has been mine so long, street
and bicycles, monuments

descend in it. In the bedroom, a shirt
has fallen on shoes. Keep me

from seeing: Moon wanting into the dark
like the torn from—

the photograph—
It is August. One woman is so long

longing does not come out of her.
But this time I have loved you

so long I become

the boy you were. I must still

be alive, for everything is changing and
incomplete. Half a tree, half

drives its shadowy web near the shutters.
August has just turned September. The ancestors

want 4000-year-old grain, hard as quartz,
in grain jars. All I have are cigarettes.

What a night this is. What a night.
I'll lie down and my pillow will thrum

like a machine. I'll go barefoot
to the window, see if any light is

still on in any house. Who else
is afraid of missing something. Who else

knows one thing God can't enter
is my memory: I, a minor

twentieth-century poet, the first
of September, 4 A.M., finish one thing.

Lie Awake Lake (2005)

Prologue as Part of the Body

It begins with something backward—
gardenia tucked behind
the ear as if scent could hear
its undoing

the fantastic bodice of a space
no larger than this plump
of sweetness, yeastlike, tropic

it begins with a turning, a trope,
that fragrance spiraling the cochlea
and the body confused by the enchantment
of the wrong orifice wrong passage—it was

after all where music should be unwinding,
cry shedding its epithelial layers, the tac-tac
of someone entreating, far away, some door . . .

But it was summer trying to enter, swoon its way
into the skull, the Parfum Fatale collapsing
on the organ of Corti

a secret island discovered by the Italian anatomist
of the last century though it was always there
in the body, the locus of quivering
like the letter M

deep in its alphabet, the humming
on either side. Beginning is

the flower to the ear
the flute to the palm, the glittering mirror to
the back of the head, the steaming rice and the plums
in honey

to the feet, to the vertebrae, to the pineal gland:

oblivion, oblivion, oblivion.

Eye

It was not by accident the eye
was attracted to the water,
the eater of doubles: the good
cattail and the bad cattail, one
rising from the other like memory—the gnat
and the gnat, the sycamore reaching up
to heaven and the sycamore hanging down
to that heaven . . . So the dizziness
that beauty is, losing
is. And with this bark-colored eye,
this eye that was a father's and
a mother's, I drank
back the helpless world—the one
that is all body, not spirit, not
a bit—that is silt, sex, and germ
and the Temple of Being Beside. I was
young beside you, water, and my father and I
were on your face, there were willows, and this
was in early summer or at least
it has become early summer,
that double of once.

Flying In

Here I am, the last
place on earth . . .

The city has everything. It has

more windows
with more lights on
in them

than any
homecoming.

Father,
you're the far away lake

the far away lake

the lie awake lake.

Open

In the city of it
how soon grief
becomes exhaustion—

buildings pain-high
sheening like lead in the March sun,
here

and there, a crust of snow.
Sometimes in the middle of dinner
I want to go to sleep.
Sometimes

in the middle of this
white, white, separating rose
I have to
shut my eyes—
unearthly civilization—

the fumes, the radios, the nervous
buses, the man at the pay phone
shouting, So you're leaving me—

hates me for hearing—
but once

the wound is open, it all
must go that way . . .

One More

Say I had
a calf
I had to guide through the city,

old snow
in the curbs and fresh
nakedness on the branches
of each

fenced-off tree along
the avenues, black man
repeating to no one, everyone,
You got a problem?

You got a problem?
Leading a dewy-eyed young
calf through the traffic,
bastards

staring into its
lake-silt eye, one

then the other,
isn't a cakewalk, isn't
a walk in the park, isn't going
anywhere

among the strange bawling
of cars, water-trucks,
horns. Here,

say to it, say to it,
one more look.

One more look and
we must go.

List

It was all new.
One day I bought birds-of-paradise.
One day I cleaned the oven.
One day I made a list.
The next

I did the list.
One day I sat out and watched
yellow burrs fall from
the sweet acacias.
I did

all the being you
I could, father,

all the rest
of this life.

The Week My Father Died

My brother, drunk, said
always remember

the day you were announced
we were putting up
a corn crib from Sears Roebuck,

Dad, me, your sister was helping,
your brother was helping
but mother

was sitting
and dad told us

you were coming
it was autumn then
always remember

it was a happy day.
But

this day, this day,
sick with grief
and mean-drunk, my brother said then:

Look in my eyes, look,
what do you see?

Death, I thought, but didn't say.

I'm dying, he said. You'll
never see me again.

But it was the drink talking.
It was the torn heart saying
both things. Lies, lies . . .

Lies to remember.
Lies to make time even

Lies to get time
even with us.

Wren

Once I fished a wren
from the pool
held it

little volt
in my hand

This I won't forget:

my mother's shoulders

I'm in the backseat
holding my brother's hand

my sister is driving

I don't have to see
anyone's face

the box of ashes
queerly heavy
like metal

like
the soaked sleeve of your sweater

long ago

the way something would rather drown
than trust

the hand that would lift it

Answer

Yes, I'd go back—

to the day
I was almost born
to the false alarm

that brought a cop
to the motel room
to wake my father

and to the night drive
through the spring snowfall

black outside
a little blue light on the dash

but it was Not
Yet—

it was Too Soon—

I was born in May,
but I would leave them there

with the breath and the April snow
with the waiting
with the beginning

my happiness
so great
I'd never come . . .

Far Away Lake

We can't get there
by road, by rope, by
wing

by time—
though time would be the way

by boat
by please please

time would be the way

then the reed-quiver
a cloud of gnats
mumbling its hypnotic suggestion

by sleep, sleep
until you say
lift my elbow   straighten
my legs

And I
straightened you in this life
like flowers

but the little water
there was
went to air
where it came from

And all my love for you
came back—
you couldn't take it where
you were going

you'd get halfway there
and then you'd drift
arms by your side

like a clock
plucked . . .

Question as Part of the Body

The essential question—
what do we ache for, what do we need, how do we get it?

or re-phrased: How do we not die?

How do we not see question as
part of the body?

Pain as. Light as.

Let's say the leaf is my body, the shoe
is my body, the city at night. And this might
lead me on

where are you is a part of my body, where are you
and where are you, my father, where are you
where is that time
you and the lake and the willow and the bright
aluminum band of the car in the distance, or is
time that part of

my little finger I can cut off, I can jab with a needle
and squeeze . . .

There is a duct in the heart named
for the man who found it, and the crypts of Lieberkuhn,
after another man

but not even the roses of the nipples have the name of a woman
and why?

And where are we women then when death
wants to call us in the flesh?

Answer wants no part of this—this
is no discussion this is the eternal
nag of the soul which is not

a ruby or fork or a fawn

but a car caught in the distance
gleaming as if it were a moment, why

not confuse distance with time, time
with location, location with mass, mass
with energy energy with heat and heat, heat
with the body which wanders itself
pinching and parting & asking not *what am I* but
am I?

and what is more furious than rubies,
and what is more than the deer who bend
drinking themselves up from themselves wavering
there at the edge of light
and load . . .

Fetish

. . . *a fetish is a story*
masquerading as an object.
—Robert J. Stoller

In ballet the foot disappears
and even the swan walks on air.

In this marvelous disguise of the body,
deception and beauty weigh

equally. Form is no dance,
though looking is, the leap

from here to
light's pink shrined upon the stage

while the music shivers. It's some winter, this
story of the foot

that later, through the stage door, walks away
in its black stiletto

the clarinetist behind watches disappear like a smaller
and smaller and smaller black champagne glass,

the mournful little toasts of desire over
and then that spectacle of bondage

as her strapped ankle withdraws into a taxi.
If this were the fairy tale,

the shoe would be in his hand, her shape—
and the shoe would be glass so that

her shape would seem to walk on air.
He'd name her Farewell.

But he'd keep her in a closet, he'd keep
for himself that image of the five red

half-moons of the toes, cozy and lingual.
He'd let that heel grind into

his breastbone, and why not, just think
of what we'll stand for in the name of love,

just think what we'll become a street for,
or a giving earth, a meadow for, a mud,

a heart-rooted grass. Think what we'll
disappear for in all our flesh, just to know

the gravity of our desire which is
always walking out, out, into distance

and then, when there's nothing
more, drawing itself up and lasting

a brief second like a circus goat
climbing a ladder, pitiable

miracle, our love, our art.

Lilies at Night

Surprise, they say in the dark.

And nothing happens.

Gazers, these
animals who sleep upright,

wax still, the wine red beauty-mark
here and there—
but so much shadow

and nothing.

Nothing wants
to be the body anymore.
Everything wants to be the soul
but something has to stay

something has to be the body.
These—

but open—
like blows in the side
glow of the kitchen,

and the eyelash, the anther, the red
vibrissa,

out
like lamps extinguished in milk,
and the corpse swearing *I will not drink urine,*
I will not eat excrement,
I will be young . . .

Flower. Ear-mouth. Flower.
foot-palm. Flower. Navel-eye.
Flower. Cock-heart.

A Dog Turns Back When You Turn Back

The desert won't get off my back
not even here in the green heart of Italy.
All night I lie awake and the cuckoos
repeat from the lindens repeat
the hours reliving themselves.
Then I lie on my back with

the desert beneath me.
My very gravity I feel depends
on this—cool wind, a flock of pansies
lighting in the window box, a flock of inks,
a flock of backward looks
you won't forget. I know

you can live in two places at once:
Whenever I go to bed the desert's there.
I say, "I thought I left you, I thought
we had it out." The desert
hardly stirs. My leg in the sheets—
the rustle of lizard
and no breeze: No matter which way

I turn the desert stretches out,
content. I say, "Goodbye."
I say, "I don't love you."
And the whole pillow exhales its
creosote, its turpentine bush,
and even moonlight full of
strange silhouettes and valleys.
I blame my eyes, and roll onto
my side and stick out
my elbow just for spite. But

you know the desert doesn't budge,
lies like a drunk who hasn't shaved,
who can't remember where he went
or how, and drinks to not
remembering—a little birthday
eternally when the sun comes up.
When the sun comes up I open one eye
and, since it's still there, flat

and littered with arms of chainfruit cholla,
"I hate you, I hate you,"
I say and nothing listens. Of course,
nothing. Though the quail
go strolling the dry arroyo down
to the bedpost. I blame
my breastbone. I blame my ear.
I blame the globe mallow
and the city of rock squirrels.
Cursed, I begin to sing.

The song goes, "Here, here
where the sea got up and left
I lie down." I blame my skin,
dry and withered and,
at that moment when the desert
drifts off into dream, I put
my hand into the blank space
beside me: out from it go
rings of terrible childhood, Sundays,
in the white glare of gravel and
dusts, a brand of endlessness
I both fear and crave in large

doses—the result of this lullaby,
this thing near death
beside me, clatter of mesquite pods
falling on one another
and the sound of paper,
the sound of shore, the song of
what was the song . . .

that lovers and ex-lovers ask
when they try to go back—
Nothing follows *them* around, no
scorpion waiting in their shoes,
no mean little needles pricking
through their clothes. "Leave me

alone, leave me alone," I cry
as if I were not already

thirsty and desolate. Blaming
my feet. Blaming my tongue.
Love is never, no matter how many times
we say it will be, any different.
I come from a brutal unbearable place
and every time, even in the trees
and grapevines terraced
in the valley, the desert sits on my chest
and begins to beat.

My Zen

One night the stars fall open—
in them bottomless doe-eyed topaz
and a floating meadow.

I am not on fire.
I am quite the ordinary December night.
The desert is clear, cars trail off mid-thought . . .

A meadow I swear is only a place
which you expect across—

something bounding, something coming, something
hopestruck.

In my childhood there was a cardboard house
whose windows opened like books—
and behind each, something

wrong, silly, like a fish or a cello
instead of a lamp or a chair. This is
what I saw—

one night there were stars and the moment
they came open, those whole atomic
lilies, petals where the arms of eons
rest . . .

They were only stars, mysteries, immortals, gas . . .
As if you could follow happiness to the end
of the world and not see where it goes.

God Body

At night he lay awake and listened to
the body, first the neck with its venous hum
its simmering monarchs of the pulse and then
oh the little rhoncus of the chest, those wings
stopped up in the lungs, the rub of plates and
the lubb-dupp of the heart. It was a jungle in there.
Not a garden. Not the beautiful fountain and
gentle thumbing of the leaves, but a hot
and saturated place, a terrible kudzu of passageways,
intercessions, and muck. In this first

tender auscultation, he was repulsed. How
was he going to go on? How to create desire?
In this first hour the whole skin smelled
like the washings of a gun. And great
microbial swarms threatened to steal it all.
But he couldn't go back to the beginning—
that was the tragedy of genesis, that was
the tragedy of desire, that was the tragedy
of body

so he kept it going. Swamp and all. He'd invent
everything to hurt or feed it. Even the little
stones to torment the kidney, or the mosquito
to fever it, or the shit of the rat to keep
the virus nearby when it slept. It was all
good, he told himself. Look at the hair, look
at the breath coming out like a lotus

listen to the bruits of the belly and the lowing
bowel. You can picture a field in all this.
You can picture a cupboard of fresh linens.
And the secret pouches of lavender . . .

Like This

You were wrong, you can't find the missing
leg or mouth or finger or eye or breast,
not here by the ocotillo or the blue torch,
the mounds where gophers have tunneled
under the prickly pear, leaving its bruised pads,
its rotted edges, though that other body might
be with you, phantom, as if you had eaten it and
then began your vigil of regret.
                                    Or, as we would say
in the vernacular, the farewell has so fucked you up
you see it everywhere, you see yourself
from a distance, bending to kiss your father
above his left breast. Not thinking then, why this,
why not his cheek, his forehead, he was tucked in bed,
naked, confused about who should turn on the lights,
though it was daylight.
                           His legs had gone
long ago, though he used to dream, he said, of a black
horse named Nancy who kicked in the stalls, kicked
in the door of the market. And he'd smile with admiration.
The next year God started on his spine. And you began
to see that any god would have to
hate the body, so transparent were its motives,
so transparent was its hope. Or, in other words, such
a mess of need and shit and swelling and shrinking
that it was a wonder it could bear itself.
                                    It could not.
These were the last days though you never know them
until after. They smelled of stale smoke inside the van
that took him back and forth to the doctor. It was an entire
day's work, getting him out of bed, onto the gurney,
getting the gurney through the narrow hall and foyer of that house,
lifting it into the van, it took the four of you, and then later,
in the clean lobby, you stood with your father lying there
as if in bed, there in front of everyone staring and then
you got to wait, wait until the doctor had time. Wait, staring
at his bare shoulders while he asked where's my wife?
Then the doctor asked him what year it was, his name,
could he go *like this* and she bared her teeth and he bared his teeth

and he knew the year, he knew his name. The next day
he died. And the doctor was surprised as if it were some
bastard miracle, the soul saying *can you go like this* and the body
going like this.
                      But, before that, after you explained the lights
didn't have to be on, it was afternoon, and he drank his juice and
you put down the cup, you leaned and kissed him on the chest,
and then you went. The breast and the breastbone
vanished. And the warm curve of his skull you used to put your hand on
and scratch his head. And then, though you were middle-aged,
the girl-body disappeared completely—there was nothing to keep her.
You cut your hair. And won't go looking. You're sure the only
thing left is breath, the animal breath. At night you lie awake and
listen. It crawls up and curls on your stomach
and with both hands you feel its ribs swell out and out. And that's
enough for now. For *now* is the word of the body.

Sly Sparrow

What they sewed me up with would dissolve
that's what they said when they stitched my breast
over the heart the cat wouldn't eat
though she'd swallow even the bones. Now
I like to study
my scar in the face of the rain puddle
not as clear
anymore as when they shaved me
the better to graft my new wing, smear
my eye with emerald jelly. That's when
I was the cooperative sparrow. Call me
Jane. But when the thread
disappeared into me like a childhood
I began to call up song like a knot.
I became one mean musical
motherfucking sparrow: Call me Nicole. Though
by nature
we are a tolerant sort, like therapists
or pears. It's when I died I became
fierce and also I missed
the leaves, those only earthly
things that used to flutter under my weight
like eyelash over dream. Those nights
I drank I couldn't stop drinking until
I gave the thirst away to anyone
in need of a thirst from God.

Diving Horse Shuffle

and juggling dogs, he said, what do you think

the sun was out with mountains holding up its tail

she was thinking

at the point where our joy is greatest why don't we die

the doctor suggested animal therapy

the couch was orange as a cigarette

she was thinking

why doesn't he swing me from his trapeze

I think dogs can't juggle, she said

the sun began to slouch losing his tail in the horizon

he was thinking

she was in love with the doctor whatsisname

like a potato in chowder

the couch was orange as a fist

why not celebrate everything she said swirling an olive

gin is the first law of gravity

look, my therapy is barking, she said

no, I mean instead of balls we juggle dogs

shit she was thinking

the orange was very much in love

the sun flopped down anywhere

here's to Fruit Loops, she said, I could suck them all night

he took out an anti-gravity Marlboro and lit up

goddam doctor

Christ awful couch

do you juggle them by their heads or their bottoms, she said

orange has no pity

"Look a firework shows/its claws raking empty space:/and the wound is gold!"—*Basho*

Basho was a great poet

like a dragon is a poet

Basho was a great poet because he never wrote these words

she was thinking, why don't we die at the moment—

the couch was a juice stain in the middle of the room

Sex in Heaven

Two curtains touching,
essential curtains, filmy and white
took me back to a window,
a particular one in memory—
you can't look in a window and not
see it—not have desire
stare back like a parting,
the gold slit through the night.
Which body to kiss with? Which age?
The curtains were willing.
That's all it took to unlock the house
from our past and the past
that was better. For we were
paradisiacal creatures—and will
create it everywhere. Oblivion's
no different: you're born
longing for home. First, it's a body.
Or before that, the body's scent.
Then it's a place. A place
that will come to you at any moment
like a kitchen light. The window,
the curtains close as breath
drawn over the shadow couple, again,
again. They believe the sea cares
for them, truly it does. And at any moment
the sea will begin to break down
and weep.

Dogwalk Triptych

1. How Long

Sometimes a dog so much enjoys being
a dog, taking the shoe in his teeth,
tossing it toward the waves and when
the shoe makes a landing, possessing it
again, grounded between his paws,
his nose in its boat, all
despite the man's protests who retakes
the shoe and sits beside him, both
looking out to sea.

The man does not enjoy so much
being a man holding a shoe while
light shuffles the sea. Now is not
his time; it is the dog's time. Time being
only the eye of the observer
who travels at some other speed as waves
lift their flanks of silver light
and roll over to eternities. Named June.
A month

is nothing a dog knows. A second,
a day, a forty-minute nap, is all
the same. Aging is nothing—it's
the waiting that confounds him.
At home, once the door closes and the man
is gone, how long?
How long is how long?
The creature alone cannot measure duration.

But the sea is the sea was the sea is
the sea. And the man is watching it like a fire,
a great blue fire, bluer than memory
when it comes to him: the song,
an old song, song of the dogmen, *shu-wa*,
who want what they love to be
still a moment, *lu-la, lu-la,*
but it never is.

2. *Topos*

A man sits in his chair on the shore and opens his book.
The dog sits on the sand and looks up at the man.
This is geometry.
Soon the man is in a world of make-believe:
In the square, the cafés full of thieves,
political assassins. The dog, left behind,

smells something dead downwind,
a bird, a baby seal . . .
Geometry. Geography. Dogography.
All of it, a point and a point and the space
between. The book

is all about a man shipwrecked so long
he attains magical powers. Above the open
book an abandoned
boogie board passes, big slapstick on the light.
The dog settles his belly in the cool sand, chin
to the wind. The man turns a page.
The next wave holds up its hand in a trance
and then walks.

Orchestra, all of it. Things coming into
other things. The dog coming certain of
the scent. Its plot. Angle and dimension.
A beautiful girl in the book is drowned
while the man sleeps.

It's the middle, the exact middle for
all concerned, and would stay that way
except that the dog
loves the man more than the man loves the dog.
And a day at the sea is a date with memory.

3. Promenade

In the end, Blackie, all our names are

writ in water. Watch the shadows now
dress themselves and walk
the shore like dogs and men, like men
and long-legged birds. They are birds and
men and dogs in another time. Another

word for this: The dog
is running and turning running and turning
as the man heads back the way he came,
his shirtback blown out and luffing
big as bread. Full sail then, two
head for home. It's how the world
should end. But the man is thinking about
his toes, how one is beginning to cross with

another and the body's story is another:
The Greeks once thought the liver was the heart
and all passion resided there.
Now love lights in the hippocampus.
But love still lights. That's the main thing,

Blackie. A dog brain or a man brain,
it's all the same. Form ends and form
goes on: The dog

looking up though shadow's dug out
his eyes. Soon he'll put on his night ears, hear
through one wave after another,
tshu-ah, tshu-ah,
the high sirens calling this world

the other, insubstantial
but eternal, its beings unseizable mists.

Blossom at the End of the Body

Leaving this world must be the flower,
its three violet faces turned to the air—a man can't look
at a flower without knowing he's dying.
That's the beauty. Parting must be this little
chance, with its stem and flutter. It's no god
and it's no force and our grief is a rock, a clod,
a punk of earth. Truth is,
what we will miss most
isn't her or him or mother or child but
the particular blue at the side of the field,
the heart's pure botany, for

the body is a science. And there is no
substitute for *thing*. Not love, not happiness,
not faith. But flower. But flower. But flower.

The Book of Accident (2006)

Twentieth Century Children

We were born in the light
of the war of the Gargantuas.
We were born into the picture
as others might be born into the world,
with the bloom of a giant ape foot
over Tokyo, with the blink of
the Lizard Men in New York. Not God,
but the God-hairs brushing close—and the fire
up first like a fat mutant
gold cicada
which had slept in the earth
on the secret installations.
We were bathed
in the glow of the beast
from 20,000 fathoms, the arctic
flash of calving ice,
our bright fur groomed
under a mother's tongue that clicked
like starlodes. We
were created in the image
of the image of the glazed
stare of God, its half-lives,
its dream-kitchens of gold-
flecked tile, its backyard
bottle trees and common wrens, its
television, television
glitter on our faces, other
on our faces, other
falling on our beds, utter
dying we were the picture of,
an eye for an eye,
an eye for a mouth.

Darkroom

Everything is in the process of recurring:
Colts in the darkroom,
those clarifying blots with jaws,
disjointed spines—

The sow from Malinovka
born without eye sockets—

These aren't our children.
Last night, she would tell him,
I gave birth to a son in my sleep.

He was an ordinary wolf boy.

But why reason with the God of Pictures?

And why say to a man, "The accident
was so long ago, why can't you forget?"

Twentieth Century Children (2)

Everything she finds she drags home:
the cat, the ruined boots, the rusted knife,
the legless doll—

Can I keep it? And the boy is packing
a snowball in the freezer to save
for August. The sisters, no wiser, are
keeping warm

some small blue eggs on a cotton ball
constellation under mother's make-up lamp.
Things will stay.

Things will wait. This child's
America cooks up forever, and the stars
get pasted in their Book of Looks—

This light.
This word.
This favored found stone they sleep with.
And the moth they've sealed in

a plastic pin box and buried beneath
their folded summer shirts, so that someday
when they leave or when

they marry, they will find it
still, thing
and no more
the dream around it—

The New Boy-Wonders

They would have found the place earlier
except the one with *Torture* spelled out on his T-shirt
was afraid of lightning,
the arm shagging after him,
its zag into white time,

Orchid Town:
kids out on the streets blossoming
their cigarette cherries,
dogs staring from the windows like mothers

wondering, What's that year slinking by the porch?

When they reintroduced us to the wild,
one said, we lost track
we forgot our movie stars
we forgot our fire-scars
we forgot poetry.

In the next flash a house stepped
onto the far hill
and the meadow was licked

clean as the face of an object—
the metal crate
the experiment slept in, hush-hush—

the wolf boy left by accident
in the middle of someone's field.

Dialogue: Memory and Forgetting

Naked and pale, pale as the plucked end of light,
is this your only body, this

you cover with mud, with fur, with sweet oil,
a sheet?

You drive it to work and back. And on the way
it comes to you, wolves

come from the book of snow
of childhood, fur taking in the weak
light, the light so low

it's important
not to know what next,

what goes out—
Here, I said,
it's a world where no one has to love you.

But they do.

Nights in the Constellation of the Twin-Hearted Prisoner

—for R.B.G

Then the body said   Did you love me   Prove you loved me.

And I said to the notebook   Nothing but you, the horizon—

And it was true.

I was thinking of the face
      my mother used to carve on the apple
      before she gave it to me to eat—

I was, as always, faithful to my memory, my very
      last . . .

And then there are dreams that become memories,
      my dream of the two prisoners with the same name—
      one in his cell, one missing

and I take the one out and put him beside
      the cell of the missing one

so they'll think he's there—and so far
      this isn't much different from memory, down

to the last detail of the man who wanders
      the prison village at night
      carrying a lamb no one will cook.

Then the body said   Take me with you.

And the childhood knife said   I will take you
      with me, I will smile

you tenderly with me, I will tend you,

the sweet evening said, I
      who wove you and weft you, I will

pour you from one breast to another,
      I will feed your missing, and the blue
      solaces said, And

where my alone meets your alone, I will,
          oh Lamb in Arms,

yes, I loved you, Husband Skin,
          husband

like guilt when I came I was yours forever.

Torture Boy's Watch, Burn Boy's Boat of Souls

What kind of boy was this
watching over the Orchid Town swannery—

He was the kind, he'd marry a girl and then say,
"I hate your mother,
your sister too, and all the shitbirds
you came from." Oh, then
you'd know the ache of love . . .

But first he'd meet the boy at the wolf-rock
lighting gasoline rags
and they'd wonder together if the story
they were in were true,

the story where the burning rag floated
across the water, and the fat tantaras
of the swans set off

a knifing lamentation in the woods
as the rag boat lit the other shore
and died—

the shape of the wolf flared out,
the shape of the boy flared out
dark,

weird as an accident in the Bible—
the chapter where God, having lost
his lover in the trees, stumbles

in verse 18
across forgetfulness . . .

Third Body

Because the past is in love the way
the future is not,
the child I abandoned
I abandoned

without language: a blood ache
this silence
like my mother's childhood,

this her, red-budded dress in my dream,
this me, this it,

this not-a-hair, not-a-whisper,
this squat—

child on its haunches, enchanted
the way the lost have to be

to be, after such a longing.

Lightning-Wolf

—*for Hershman John*

Then the wolf-boy was living
in a metal crate in a snowbound pen
in someone's field.

Spring came.
It came through a hole in the top of the crate.
Heady as the vanilla bogs,

east, which belonged to
the Conservator of the Meadow.
And the ice melted

all at once with the hiss of a bootstruck match,
with a large and sloppy kiss—
The crate floated like an ark
and there were showers,
thunder,

and the 4000-volt bolt belting
the glitter-to-shit out of the bright box
and he was born again

crackling by his short hairs,
a life so quick it was
memory before it passed,
pissed itself

before the body. As before the executioner
throws the switch.

As before the animal
finds the door.

How He Became Conservator of the Meadow

The meadow used to take care of itself,
the parting and lying down,
the bending and silvering,
the propagation of yarrows—

the visitation of wings,
the mimicry of sashes in the dusky hour,
and the clammy perfumes that came

from the opening and shutting of spaces.
He could feel, as night was
coming through, the meadow
holding his feet. This was before
the song sparrow became extinct,

and the blue pike,
and the ruby terror-flower,
the pride of June. And before

there was shopping nearby and
a fireworks factory—so suddenly it seemed
that a man born in the twentieth century
could not finish his pastoral elegy . . .

Torture Boy at the Easter Confest, Repentance Creek

The year Jimmy had four pearls
inserted in the shaft of his cock,
Torture Boy took tusks carved from pau-pau shell
and pierced them through his upper lip,
wore them for five days before
his gums were too eroded, and signed
the Mutation Manifesto anyway. Outer
Change is Inner, would say the goddam
T-shirt. He'd laugh and then begin
to worry that when he laughed he was
ugly.

There was a bluebird one morning,
something he'd never seen, and
it made him gasp. What a girl
I am, he thought, and put beetles
in all the sleeping bags and, in
Jimmy's, itching powder. That
made him laugh

and that made him ugly.
And that made him want to hang himself
and come.
        Instead, he took his knife
down to the creek where he'd think
of the old lady living in a cabin
down the road. She'd always smile
and give a little wave in that old
lady way that pissed him off.

When it got dark, yeah, he'd buzz
past her place on his dirtbike,
then back nice and close and then
around the fucking house. He'd scare her
before he'd use the knife to cut
a lock of hair first
then all her stupid old lady buttons.
Yeah. She'd
cry. He'd want to be merciful,

so he'd explain how the way back

was light already, the water so cold
it stung his face awake. She'd understand
he was just an instrument. He was good.
Felt fresh, fresh as the day he was born.
Yeah. And they'd laugh . . .

Life Story

When I read to the wolf boy,
he fell asleep right during the part
the kingdom's sky began to brood and
lightning jimmied the great amethyst doors
open through the dark—

He dreamed there was a village
of things ajar that sons peeped out from,
and he could see
the women in their kitchens
making wolf pie.

And if he woke,
they'd die, and if he slept until morning,
they'd forget,

the ovens would cool . . .
or something burning

would follow his life burning, and he'd
turn, and he'd never quite see
what it was—

fairy tale, fairy tale,
memory or recipe,

musk in the mouth,

I snap off his lamp into
his breath—ah,

small leaving thing,
the rain isn't falling—
it is cleaved.

Nights in the Constellation of the Tree Stepping from its Robe

—for Norman

Like a star or a stick suddenly given
the way to say everything it held in so long,
the leaves fall
open from the tree, says the dream, like yellow kimonos . . .

Thank God here
we're the only ones who speak,

not the wooden chest, the blue ginger-jar lamp,
not the shoe going under the bed,
not the tree stepping from its robe,
though it seems if anything had the right . . .

I wake from where
there's no such thing as mute. Each thing has

its lament, its refrain,
its sustaining gibberish.
Oh kiss and kiss and kiss, says the boat
floating from that dock of rickety dark . . .

And only now
I feel ashamed, burning off
that word-life, as if only now
the quiet room can hear again.
Nothing says, welcome. Nothing says, lost,

adrift, daft, bedizened, daughter—
though I've come
from that country
where the simple sheet of paper whispered,
Bread. And bread

said, Mist.
And last—

Last night the *shochet's* axe poured its blessing over
the hen's stretched neck:

Between poetry and justice, choose justice,
between poetry and desire, choose desire,
between poetry and death,
choose death, because you have no choice.
Only when there is nothing else,
fight for poetry.

The Life and Times of Skin Girl

1.

She decided to follow the gods home
in their gownlike T-shirts and shaved skulls.

Twilight was still a feather.

The blood pumped hard in their radio,
it said, sex kings sex kings

as objects turned to their blueness slowly
and, slowly, the world of the eye was leaving
and coming into the world of the hand . . .

Soon she lost the toss of their shadows
in the calving darkness,

the last shrew cricket falling finally off
the night's steep magnitudes.
And suddenly, there,

at the corner, they went in. And were nightingales.
Where was the field of mercy?
Where were the ambrosial drops in
the cup of hours?

Midnight: One light so shimmery
they had to undress for it—

all nipple and seam and near human.

They had stopped
singing. Could be birds no more. Took off
their soft

sleeves, took out the silver
beads from their tongues . . .
and the beads like seeing beings sat.

2.

As if she'd gone down into the dead,
there was no one to come and lead her back.

But all the light she'd need was at
their fingertips: One with his thumb
scratched the matchhead alive, threw

the flame to the floor where it blueballed out.
This, he said,
for the bitch who thought my world too dark
and frightening, too atomic and unkind . . .

That's all she'd need to fall in love with death—
to believe he was merely misunderstood

while his minions lay on mattresses,
snakes on their backs.
Roses.
Lightning bolts.

What time was it?
Where was the well to bring up infant souls?
Truant waters . . .
Mostly they slept and reminisced and sailed
their brief matches in the lap of blackness.

It was a game of dedication: This, one said,
for the bitch who put words in my mouth.

3.

She could smell weed and clove
and see one of them coming to the window
by the Day-Glo alien doll
hung around his neck. It was green
as ice. He,

the void over which its small face moved.

And the void was the night
she passed out in the railroad tracks among the cellophanes

the candy-ravers crushed and left,
and the Star Express came roaring. The night

that Lala Petite had stuck her head in
a woofer during the dope rave at the Nile.
That night the gods so loved the world
they let

anyone in for five bones and
then let the One Singing lift her up
to the light at the mouth of the place—candles

shrining a framed picture of the Dalai Lama.
And then the train.
A thousand lamas blazing.

4.

Looking is the only great thing the gods do.
Otherwise, sheer boredom. Sheer world.
Same transparent ache of having
named everything. Everything being their child,
their dumb, deaf child.

It is this way: Everything
in the window is out the window.
Her face

leafed slowly through the black air
as his eye turned her—sight
and memory shuffling

the looked-upon. She moved back.
The remembered-after.

She turned.
The looked-after.

That feeling of streaming from looking.
That whole gold snakedom—

5.

When she finally stopped running and was
seated in the stiff orchidean light of
the Pancake House, halos hunched over
two stacks and a side as she watched

the boy in the hairnet turn back into steam
until nothing was left but the luminous
patch of the coffee cup and the whole
pleasing punk of the place . . .
the house music, breakbeat and trance—

She looked out
into the drosophilas' frenzy like some
weird fizz up the picture glass.

It was the nightmare of the seconds.

6

The spirits: How is it to live in the world?

The bodies: Who lives in the world?

White moment of the morning, that cool-sheeted air and not having slept.
And not having slept, she felt she had come from somewhere secret and distant
and not entrusted to just anyone.

The parking lot set with tourmalines.

And not entrusted to anyone.

There were times when the light felt like a look, just taking in her face, dwelling on her hair.

This was as good as a god gets.

The god being
one who never turns around.

Body of the Hour

To say, *the soul*

is like saying, *the clock*
lost its body and went on ticking.

Shadow-body, this one
who lived behind the bat-faced
bone of the pelvis

raised in the slicked-back hackle of blood . . .

To say, comfort me now in the hour
of my loss is

to be the hour, always.
To be Lord Almost.
Mother So-Close.

To be this time each time
you stop—put down the fork
or turn the page and look up:

The meadow in a lather of white
four-o-clocks, the birthmarked
butterfly moving

as if written—erased—written . . .

I remember once in this world
I was an absence,
like you. Like you.

Annunciation

They say it happened
during unauthorized experiments by the operators.

They say conception
was a draught of wind, the will
of an angel blew the dome off
the reactor.
                    The countryside was drunk at the time.
Bulls staring at the usual walls while,

for a moment, the whole of April had gone
female around them . . .
When at last

a witness showed up, the windows were
knocked out, the old maternity hospital

was littered with glass and metal instruments
too radiant to touch—
wormwood bushes blackening over the steps—

It's the way new lovers
say it happened: like a blinding, like a blast.
And yet all through it someone
was able to write poetry. And later,
someone came to record,

to interview the old woman and photograph
her goat-mule,
the freak offspring of the abandoned farms—

She said, in rough translation,
Who you turn to
when your town burns up,
                    well, that tells you everything.

The Torture and Burn Boys Entered the Video Arcade

Move over, geek—
they said, This is our game.

The lights blinking like candies, red
cinnamon buds and silver drawer pulls
and bright green fizz-beans

timed to the electric yips and cha-bongs
of some genius with an earring in his eyebrow
kicking cyberass

and saving Skull Lord.
The boys were hot—
it was a holiday,
the Feast of Yarrows—
hands on the joysticks

exploding blue strobe-finches from
the fallout of the pixels and the trees,

Burn Boy flipping back his satin bangs,
all twitch now, playing
Baked Revenge, Kingdom of O's, Heartstopathon.
Then Buzzarding the Meadow—

Again, and again twice.
Beat that—

and the other said,
Watch this, fucker.

And he said, Yeah, I'm shakin'.

So he said, Bite my big one. And
he said, Fuck you. Then
the other said, Fuck you. So he
said, Fuck you,

and the brotherhood was complete
and not long

after their starry numbers came up:
24 kills apiece, the all-time
third-highest

after 25 scored by player Ezra LB.,
and the record,
29, held by the player who went by the name,
Wolf Boy,
King of Thebes . . .

Twentieth Century Children (4)

One night sitting around the meteor pit
outside town, she swore
she could smell the afterlife, this
earth gashed by stars—

out there,
what was left but the insect whine
of boys' dirt-bikes seaming the field . . .

She could imagine their far-off swoons of dust
and the zinc taste of their mouths
and what their souls would look like

if there were souls—
like gray tufts of fur snagged on barbed wire—

and then remembered
on such and such a night, so much later,
as if she'd been missing since childhood
and suddenly—

here,
the gorge of solitude . . .

The Fourth Body

And suddenly—
here,
the gorge of solitude . . .

as if she'd been missing since childhood
and then someone said,
You've blossomed.

And the night's spring rush:
I have so much to tell you!

(Was my father a wolf or a man)
(Was my mother a mother or a dream)

So now if I tell you I stand here,
my hands
through the sleeves of the body,

the fourth body—
I can tell you you have no
idea what is the personal

white wolf until
you've seen autumn standing there

—in your place—

holding his purplish scrotum like a sack of leaves.

The Set Glistening

It was then I thought I heard someone
say there were birds in the library.
I knew it was autumn.

I knew in such a season
books were flying open, open

for days and then suddenly shut
like rooms into which half

a heated argument has gone.
I was wrong.

I had misheard the voices completely.
The only real understanding was in
the cocked head of the crow
pacing the green car's rooftop

as I walked a little farther and
everything became a little later,

time and distance, the ribs of the encyclopedias,
the pushiness of the whispers,
hush, you're not supposed to

be fully alive yet: This is the place of books,
the shooting up, the twittering, the preening,
the middle-of-the-night and fabulous

concatenating calls, song slipknotting
the egregious minutes, the cooling dark—
It was then

I had nothing left to bless but my own mistake,
not a logical thing

like the soul, smart enough not to inhabit
the body, but living in the nearby

rock or owl and eating at its separate table.
And the time, as it is set glistening on that table

is different from the time we wait for
over here.

There was a time when there were scarlet
tanagers rustling behind the shelves,
and the Russian poets

left at their table, one still asking,
Who shall I tell my sorrow,
my horror greener than ice?

Sometimes I have nothing left to praise
but someone's sorrow.

Which is like my sorrow, which is like
the perfect and severe whistle of the bird
smart enough

to stay out of our heads—stay up all night
reciting the law codes

which it does from pure memory,
greener than ice. In the deep

accident of my ear. Mine alone,
the joy of surviving twice the same
mistake—

one more time and no one will remember
that wasn't the way it went,
the original song, it went like

the larks were stars and the mountains
were Bibles and whatever was said
was said between them.

Nights with the Star-Ladle over the House

Who now
leaves the door open a crack,
the hall light, the mother light,

the Light-All-Night
planting its straw of sleep?

Don't be sad when the drifting begins,
no one to talk
water to the glass,
rim to the window.

It's an ordinary life—
And to this angel

the whole body is throat.

And the two worlds—
are they still there, world

of the guarded, world of the guard—

First you're one,
then you're the other.
But you're the other the longest . . .

That's what the light meant.

Twentieth Century Children (5): Blood-Kissing

The boy in the girl's ear says, Kiss me until
  you draw blood.

And she's the hot thorn on his lip.

Stars wince and swell and wet,
  endless little cut-me's . . .

Through the night the great sponge of traffic,
  the oozy distance, the radios, the malls,
  the cat survivalists

living out of a hole in the library.
Someone

has to say it: Nail me
  to you.

The girl has always loved like suicide.

And the kiss wants to
  know, Am I deep enough—

Am I lord and cock-ring
  and ruby hammer,

spike and sundering thing?

The black place in the skull saying,
  Infect me. Be not only *Other*
  but *It*.

The way desire is—
  live rat sewed up inside us.

Summer Heats Like the Needle in its Chosen Skin

And hummingbirds flung into the air,
fistful of violet amphetamines—

The clear water of the sky
as it dusks.

The ground, the road tar, the rock,
as if they know fever, know
the mouth that keeps coming

to the belly—
wolf-mouth

and the boy who shimmers out
on the balcony tonight blinking
strychnine and gold tracers,
passion vine

staring in the pool those blossoms
never come up from,
little humanities . . .

Let's go out in the desert and shoot things,
June Boy says.

Let's tie up a dog on the freeway.

Watch
the lights trying to say *turn away*,
burn away

to the stink of ethanol and piss.
As if mystery

was asking for it.

Washed in the River

Of course the woman with the mouse-child was famous,
as grace is famous,
a rarity

at the end of suffering. She kept him in
a nest in the dry bathtub
and washed in the river.

And though only children were meant
to believe this, I still believe this.
The fate of the body
is to confound

itself with everything. That's why
in another tale, the fair sister
opened her mouth and spoke
rubies,
and the plain sister, vipers and toads.
Meanwhile, the mother

of the gray thing
bathed him in a teacup.
Plucked him out and let him
run along the shore

to the window. Where both of them
were struck in longing—
he behind the great glass,
she behind the gray boy.

The second you see yourself in the suffering
the story's over.

And One More New

There is a Rock in Tent City

—for Bruce

The way is dark, this story begins
and won't apologize. Because I enter
the corridor between the chain link fences,
their skeletal garlands of barbed wire
and the moon behind the cloud it proves
and because there, at the end, the gate's
worse than a symbol. Again, tonight, I'm back on time.
None of my business which fat officer who's chosen
this life unpadlocks and swings the gate open
as we drop our cigarettes like tails
and file in, toss our plastic bags of glasses, keys,
change, short pencils, on the table, slip out of our shoes
and assume The Position. The gate clangs shut.
Then it's just time again, eleven at night and 105°,
still. Still. *Let's see the bottoms of your feet.*
After nineteen days you still don't know what
or how or when but that someone is going
to fuck with you. And you're going to say
Yes Ma'am, Yessir, Yes Officer. And you're going
to be thinking, Fuck Off, Suck This, Eat Me,
Bitch. But you've left your face out there, mouth
with the dark and food and solitude, those mysteries,
they're not even your real feet
sliding back into your shoes that walk the Yard,
bright with light all night, every night, not even
the wet towel you hang on your jail face as you
lie in your bunk can quench it. After twenty-six
days I've begun to miss terribly the invisible.
I've become tender toward clichés. Gotten used to
lock down, know when to disappear the plastic bottle
wedge it between the metal beam and canvas of the tent
to give the heat it holds three inches more to travel
before it hits my skin. If I forget, the D.O. with the big
belt and tight bun will threaten to Roll Me Up: No
work release, job lost, you vanish from Tent City
to more hot days in stripes, the inmate's baggy jumpsuit,
your underwear, the Sherriff's brainstorm, jail pink. I'll never

see my life and all because of something so banal
it's hard to see how it could hurt. But you think anyway
about these things on sweltering days with nowhere
to go but in your own brain. Tomorrow, Saturday,
will be scorching. By afternoon no one will even move.
No one will know it's Sunday. Same heat, same soaked
towels, same gagging odor when it's night, flesh
burning in the crematorium at Animal Control.
It's the building you see through the south fence
across from the jail cafeteria. North side's
the Towers where the sex offenders bang the walls
whenever we women walk the Yard. They
are cool in there. We envy them. One dusk
a silhouette, three windows up, waved. My instinct
was to wave back, but I made myself turn
away. And not because we were warned
but because it seemed somehow less cruel
that hour the darkness would try to fall and I'd
imagine myself out of here and only get as far as seeing
my body turn into that corridor at curfew, stand
a moment where a few rescued horses shifted in the stalls
making a music sometimes when the feeding bucket
knocked its metal against the bars I couldn't quite
make out. What kind of world was it if this place
was refuge? Last night the dust devils kicking up and
blowing through the tents, the air too close, I remembered
the name I'd heard an inmate who cleaned the stalls call
as I was passing. *Whoa there, Jed.* The palomino
lifted his head, replied with a nicker, a sound
which could have been, for all I knew, his way
of saying back the inmate's name: *Ho there, 51-03.*
I'm 65-19, my tent, my bunk, where I kill the nights
trying not to be here. We're allowed one magazine
or one softcover book. I thought at first of some escapist
thriller, or something fat like Tolstoy, and for a while
had luck with someone's discarded paperback on Buddha
as I was beginning to understand what was
an eternity. If you count the days here,
it's too slow—all waiting is identical. The mind
too flatlined to stay with much, I'd drift

to melancholies or squint down the white desert light,
watch Inca doves who'd built a nest in the looped
barbed wire. If you toss them a crumb and are caught,
you can kiss your ass goodbye, *rolled up*
means not even your own underwear will go where you go
and I hear where some bitch might
decide to slam your head into a rock because
she's missing her afternoon *novelas*, or she's tired of
the puke they serve at chow. We like to think
we're stronger than this, that we'd have the spirit
to survive the worst. But this place strips you down until
you only know one thing and that
is that you don't know who you are without the things
you call your life. I met my jailself as three women
carried 40 lb. bags of ice to fill the cooler, the melt
our only water. A novice had dumped the old ice on the ground
and they were chiding her for waste but I had run
already to the bathroom had grabbed
the plastic trash bag and returned and, scooping
the brilliants back up into it, was wrapping my jail towel
around it, and heading to the tents before a D.O. could
come out. Then they, too, began
to seize their chance. That so far was my enlightenment.
By afternoon it reached 119°, and we saw the same hour
passing and starting over, passing again until the wild
pink sun lay low behind the blank gray buildings beyond
the fence, and carts stacked with styrofoam containers
were wheeled into the Yard. The same
hot slop as every evening, and every evening
wasted: Bodies sleepless, glazed, were waiting
to be reborn back into their human lives
which were good mostly before we fucked them up
though, by now, I'm no longer sure it wasn't a dream,
sitting in the living room, or walking into the kitchen,
or someone briefly looking up from the TV as you
come home. I'd begin again to walk
toward the gate, lingering by the stalls, my last
smoke chasing the smell of pissed-on straw and fields

near Fresno I'd driven by one summer. This time
I'd leave the Buddha unfinished, and bring a poet
named Larry, because he grew up by those fields, because
his heart blew out, and because I thought his silence came
too soon. Until I understood it was the voice
and not his name this tired horse broke his knock-kneed
stance for, though I said it anyway, hey boy, hey Jed,
shining in my sweat while down that corridor
the men let in the gate turned facing out,
the bald D.O. patting them down then peeling off
his blue latex gloves which dropped dead to the cement.
Here, the burro's kneeled in the next stall, the palomino
breathes my fingers hooked through the fence links,
right here, in the heart of the five square blocks of county
correctional facilities. I want to tell Jed the Buddha's
wrong, we never choose the world
we live in. But he is still, stands holding me in
his left eye. The men behind the gate have left that empty space
we call the dog run. It was one of them, I think, who said
ten months ago when he went in, the horses were sunken, skin
and coat. Now, they look American. The way
is dark. Tonight, there's little difference I can tell
between the cruel and the kind, except that one has
a longer memory. And this story depends on which.

Acknowledgments

Grateful acknowledgment is made to journals and magazines in which these poems first appeared:

Alaskan Quarterly Review, The American Poetry Review, The Antioch Review, The Black Warrior Review, The Clackamas Literary Review, Columbia Review, Crazyhorse, Field, The Gettysburg Review, Gulf Coast, Hayden's Ferry Review, Harper's, The Indiana Review, The Iowa Review, The Journal, Lake Effect, Manthology, The Massachusetts Review, Michigan Quarterly Review, Natural Bridges, Nimrod, Ploughshares, Poetry East, Poetry Northwest, Tendril, The Virginia Quarterly Review, Sojourner, Swink, Washington Square, Western Humanities Review, Willow Springs, Autumn House Anthology, American Alphabets: 25 Contemporary American Poets, The Best American Poetry 1995, Pushcart Prize XXIII: Best of the Small Presses.

Thanks also to Cleveland State University Press, University of Akron Press, and Oberlin College Press.

The title phrase "reliquary fever" is drawn from the poem "Elegy," (c) 1980, 1994 by David St. John. Used by permission of the author.

.

Beckian Fritz Goldberg holds an M.F.A. from Vermont College and is the author of six volumes of poetry, *Body Betrayer* (Cleveland State University Press, 1991), *In the Badlands of Desire* (Cleveland State University, 1993), *Never Be the Horse* (University of Akron Press, 1999), *Twentieth Century Children* (Graphic Design Press, Indiana University, 1999), *Lie Awake Lake* (Oberlin College Press, 2005), and *The Book of Accident* (University of Akron Press, 2006).

Her work has appeared widely in anthologies and journals including, *The American Poetry Review, The Best American Poetry 1995, Field, The Gettysburg Review, Harper's, The Iowa Review, New American Poets of the 90's* and *The Massachusetts Review*. She has been awarded the Theodore Roethke Poetry Prize, *The Gettysburg Review* Annual Poetry Award, The University of Akron Press Poetry Prize, the Field Poetry Prize, and a Pushcart Prize. Goldberg is currently Professor of English at Arizona State University.